Marriage, Divorce and Remarriage

Donnie V. Rader

Guardian of Truth Foundation
C E I Bookstore
220 S. Marion St. • Athens, AL 35611
1-855-492-6657

Marriage, Divorce and Remarriage

by Donnie V. Rader

© **Guardian of Truth Foundation** First Edition, 1989; Second Edition, 1992; Third Edition, 2003. All rights reserved. No part of this book may be reproduced in any form without written permission from the publisher. Printed in the United States of America.

ISBN 10: 1-58427-079-9

ISBN 13: 978-158427-079-9

Guardian of Truth Foundation
C E I Bookstore
220 S. Marion St. • Athens, AL 35611
1-855-492-6657

Table of Contents

Lesson   **Page**

1: Introduction to the Study 7

2: Understanding Marriage and Other Important Terms 13

3: Matthew 19:9 (1) 21

4: Matthew 19:9 (2) 31

5: Who Can Marry? The Difference in the Marriage and the Bond 39

6: Death Only Cause For Remarriage 47

7: Divorce For Any Cause Without Remarriage, Divorce and Remarriage For Any Cause and Separation 55

8: Mental Divorce 65

9: Can the Guilty Party Remarry? 75

10: 1 Corinthians 7:15 83

11: Does Matthew 19:9 Apply to Non-Christians 91

12: Must Adulterers Separate? Or, Are Adulterous Marriages Washed Away at Baptism 101

13: A Review, A Look at a Few Basic Points To Remember and Conclusion 109

Appendix 113

Foreword

The subject of this study is of critical importance. The foundations of family life in America have been crumbling for the past few decades and the scourge of divorce, with its attendant evils, has grown to epidemic proportions. What once was viewed as an exception to the norm, has now become the norm. Society once frowned upon divorce. Now it is commonplace. School teachers across America tell me that they have few children in classes with the same last name as their parents. They now have step-mothers or step-fathers, most of which are the result of divorce and remarriage. No fault divorces have simplified the process in most of our states.

Sadly, the people of God have been greatly affected by this evil. We often encounter the problem in personal Bible studies. Within congregations there are cases of divorce and remarriage, some with scriptural cause and others without such cause. Over the years, good brethren have differed over various aspects of the subject and its application. Men of influence and great ability have not always agreed on this subject. People in a questionable marriage can nearly always find some preacher who will say what they want to hear.

The subject is most sensitive. It involves the lives and emotions of many people. One could hardly find a family now that has not been affected by this tragedy in one way or another. It is all too easy to allow sentiment to overshadow truth.

It is urgent, therefore, that Christians everywhere be instructed as to just exactly what the text of Scripture has to say on this matter. To that end, Donnie V. Rader has produced an excellent work for class study. He has taken great care in the production of this work to be faithful to the text of Scripture. He is a devout man and committed to the truth of the word of God. He is neither ashamed nor afraid to stand where the Bible does on this, or any other, subject. Because of the many false notions extant on this question, it was necessary to go into considerable detail in some sections of this work. Those who teach this material need to be mature and possessed of good judgment. It is possible that some points in the study may give rise to animated discussion. If all teachers and students will approach this study with an earnest desire to know and then practice exactly what the Bible teaches, great profit will come from the effort. High school and college age classes could especially benefit from this study. It might help such students to prevent some of the tragedies which others have experienced. Young married people need the study to impress upon them the permanency of marriage. Older Christians need it also, not only for their own marriages, but also in the event that some of their children or grandchildren should be caught up in the sin of remarriage without scriptural cause.

We believe brother Rader has rendered a valuable service in the production of this work and commend it to all into whose hands it might fall. Study with an open mind, an open Bible, and a determination to follow the truth of the text wherever it might lead.

Connie W. Adams
Brooks, Kentucky

Preface

As long as there are men who teach error, there will be a need for us to teach the truth and correct those misconceptions.

This book does not address a discussion of the home and how to prevent divorce and keep the home together. Other books by other authors deal with that. This volume is designed to deal with the question: what does the text say about divorce and remarriage? This work is the fruit of several years of study. My purpose from the beginning has been to set forth the simple teaching of our Lord on this subject and refute the erroneous concepts that some brethren advocate.

I publish this fully conscious that it has some imperfections (e.g. there may be some statements that are not as clear to the reader as they are to the author). I regret that it is not humanly possible to completely remove those and produce a better book.

I have tried to maintain a balance of simplicity for the common man and thoroughness for those diligently seeking answers to the questions and arguments of the day. Many get discouraged before they even start studying the question of divorce and remarriage. They may think *(1) It is too difficult, or (2) All the questions cannot be answered anyway.* This writer is convinced, the more he studies, about the simplicity of what the text says on divorce and remarriage.

I must admit that there are a few sections in this book (less than ten paragraphs in the whole book) which will be difficult for the average reader. I encourage you to bear with that, realizing that such is not the tone of the entire publication. I do believe that some "weighty" material is needed to accomplish our goal of answering many of the questions and arguments that are made.

My objective has been to produce a study book that could also be used as a workbook. It would best serve the class and the material to study it on a twenty-six week schedule.

Care must be taken when using this material (and in selecting the teacher) for a class. The issues that surround divorce and remarriage are highly controversial. The result could be tragic if it is not handled properly. Since the lessons cover as much material as they do, my suggestion is that the teacher just pick out the high points of the chapter to review in the class period and not try to dwell on all the details.

For those who want to study the question further, I suggest these works: *Marriage Is Honorable* by Gene Frost, *Marriage, Divorce and Remarriage* by Maurice W. Lusk, III, *Dabney-Frost Debate, The Bales Position Explained and Denied* by Jerry Moffitt, *Smith-Lovelady Debate* and *"And I Say Unto You"* by James O. Baird. These are just a few of the many books that have been helpful in my study.

I must express appreciation to several who have been helpful in getting this ready to publish. I thank Connie W. Adams for proofreading the manuscript and offering many valuable suggestions. I thank Gene Frost for encouraging me to finish this book, offering suggestions during the writing and critiquing the manuscript. My thanks also to H. E. Phillips, Rick Duggin, Leon Mauldin and my dad, Dorris V. Rader, for reading the manuscript and offering suggestions. The greatest thanks goes to my wife, Joan, for her patience and encouragement as I worked on this material.

I must give credit to Gene Frost and J.T. Smith for the basic ideas in a few of the charts used in lessons 4, 5, 8, 9, and 12.

I trust that you will give this material careful and honest consideration. Divorce and remarriage is not a trivial matter. It is serious business. It involves sin and salvation.

Donnie V. Rader

Preface to the Third Edition

The first edition of this book was printed in 1989, the second was published by Religious Supply Center (Louisville, KY) in 1992. I'm thankful that brethren have found the book useful enough to require a third printing. In addition to those men mentioned above, I want to thank Mike Willis for his work in editing this edition.

I would add a couple of books to the recommended list for those who want additional material on the issue. *Is It Lawful? A Comprehensive Study of Divorce* edited by Dennis Allan and Gary Fisher is worth reading. Also, the *Halbrook-Freeman Debate* provides a good discussion of the issues.

May God bless us all as we continue to study this important issue.

Donnie V. Rader
September 2002

Lesson 1

Introduction to the Study

A verse to remember: *"There is a way that seemeth right unto a man, but the end thereof are the ways of death"* (Prov. 16:25).

The loose and casual attitudes that are rampant among brethren have prompted me to prepare this book. I stand amazed at the ignorance that abounds on divorce and remarriage. Thus, every Christian needs to study what the Bible says about it. First, we need to give some attention to some introductory matters.

The Need for This Study

If one would take a look at what is going on in the world and even among brethren, he would see the need for such a study. The divorce rate is alarming. If the statistics tell us anything, they say America has a problem that deserves some attention.

Problems over Divorce and Remarriage

None should be so blind as to think that the church isn't bothered by this problem. In fact, the body of Christ has been plagued with this for many years. Yet, I am afraid that it is getting worse. We are seeing more and more members of the church getting divorced and remarrying. It is nothing uncommon to hear of some preacher, elder, deacon, or prominent member whose marriage has been destroyed.

We face serious problems as we make new converts. Many potential converts have been divorced and remarried and some of them more than once. Questions then must be answered. Are they scripturally married now? Must they separate? What was the reason for the previous divorce(s)? The same issues must be addressed with reference to those who come from other places to place membership.

Divorces are obtained for any and every reason possible. This is true even among brethren. "Incompatibility" is a very common reason. "Irreconcilable differences" is another. And, of course, many are still divorcing for the cause of "fornication."

This subject of divorce and remarriage is obviously controversial among brethren. Many brethren are teaching some very strange views on the subject — anything from the idea that there can be no divorce and remarriage to the theory that all divorcees can remarry without sin. Any time the subject is discussed, controversy is bound to arise.

Brother H.E. Phillips said it well,

The marriage, divorce and remarriage issue will probably never be resolved for all. It is not because the Word of God is not clear on the matter, nor does the real issue hang upon the definition of some words used in the Bible. The issue is difficult to resolve because of human involvement and situations with emotional overtones that cry out for some favorable answer from the Word of God to justify that human element. Many doctrines reign from the same "background" ("Introduction" to *Smith-Lovelady Debate i*).

Actually, the teaching on divorce and remarriage in the New Testament is rather easy. If one can remember three or four basic points (which are emphasized in Lesson 13), he has about all there is to know on the subject. It is imperative that we have a good knowledge of what the Bible teaches on divorce and remarriage.

What Standard Shall We Use?

One of the biggest problems we have over this issue is an appeal to unscriptural standards to determine what we believe. Let's consider a few of these false standards.

1. Family situations. There is always someone who seeks to justify some family member who has gotten himself in a mess. That situation then becomes the standard of what he believes. Many brethren change their views when a son, daughter, or themselves are divorced and remarried. I have been asked, "You mean to tell me that, if you had a son or daughter in that situation, you wouldn't think they could divorce and remarry?" Friends, our family situations do not change what the Bible says. When we determine what we believe by some family member's situation, we respect that person more than God. Jesus said, "If any man come to me, and hate not his father, and mother, and wife, and children, and brethren, and sisters, yea, and his own life also, he cannot be my disciple" (Luke 14:26). Suppose some family member never obeys the gospel. Shall we use that as a standard to say that baptism is not essential to salvation? What if a son or daughter becomes a homosexual? What right thinking parent would try to justify that? Would the family situation become the standard of what is believed?

Family situations differ. If we allow them to become our standard, then what would be right for one, would be wrong for another. We must plead for the law of God and not our families.

2. Emotions. Our reaction to truth is sometimes pragmatic. Some decide what they believe based on whether or not they like the consequences. So often on this issue, brethren respond to what is taught, saying, "That doesn't seem fair," "This doesn't make sense to me," or "That just can't be right."

There are some things that don't seem fair and right. When I read from Ezra 10, I see that God required his people to separate from the wives that they had taken from the people of the land. Ezra said, "Ye have transgressed, and have taken strange wives, to increase the trespass of Israel. Now therefore make confession unto the Lord God of your fathers, and do his pleasure: and separate yourselves from the people of the land, and from the strange wives" (vv. 10-11). Some of these people even had children (v. 44). Does that seem fair for God to make them split their families? Another example is when God held all of Israel back in their attack against Ai because of Achan's sin (Josh. 7). I can hear some of the Israelites crying now, "That's not fair!" Or what about those who would bear the consequences of their ancestors' sins (Exod. 34:7)? Do you think they thought it really fair? Suppose you had been Abraham when God commanded you to offer your only son (Gen. 22). Would it seem fair for God to ask such of you?

While these things may not seem fair and right, they are fair and right because God said they are. And it may be true that some of God's requirements concerning divorce and remarriage don't seem fair, but they are fair because God gave them! If we could see things from God's perspective, we would see the righteousness and fairness of his ways.

Truth is not always easy to swallow. Sometimes it's hard to accept. Who said that Christianity would be easy? The Lord only promised that it would be worth the sacrifice.

There will be some things in God's plan that don't make sense to us. When the man of God told Naaman to go wash seven times in the river Jordan, that didn't make sense to him at first. So he refused. He wondered why another river wouldn't do just as well (2 Kings 5:10-14). Whether or not it made sense to Naaman wasn't the point; God had commanded him to do so.

At the time that Israel was troubled by fiery serpents, God commanded Moses to put a serpent of brass on a pole so that whoever would look upon it would live (Num. 21:4-9). Did that sound like the sensible way to cure snake bites? On another occasion God instructed Israel to march around the city of Jericho for six days and seven times on the next day and then blow the trumpets and shout (Josh. 6:1-7). Obviously, this was not the normal way of taking a city. Did it make sense? Probably not to many of them. The only real sense it made (and needed to make) was that God commanded it. That's all that mattered.

NOTES

Jesus put clay in the eyes of a blind man and told him to go wash in the pool of Siloam (John 9:6-7). How on earth could that heal him? The only sense it made was that it was a commandment of Jesus.

It is interesting that so many people are opposed to regulations and laws that they don't understand. Though we may not understand or make sense of what God requires, we are still bound to do what he says. A child may not always understand why his parents tell him to do certain things. However, he is obligated to obey anyway. Do some think one is only obligated to obey the laws and regulations he fully understands and appreciates?

It doesn't change God's law to tell of some alcoholic who beats his wife and then conclude that God allows divorce for some other cause than fornication.

Man is not at liberty to decide for himself what is fair and right. Jeremiah, the prophet, said, "It is not in man that walketh to direct his steps" (Jer. 10:23). The reason is that God's ways and thoughts are higher than our ways and thoughts (Isa. 55:8-9). God is infinitely smarter than we are. "There is a way that seemeth right unto a man, but the end thereof are the ways of death" (Prov. 16:25). One must learn to "trust in the Lord with all thine heart; and lean not unto thine own understanding. In all thy ways acknowledge him, and he shall direct thy paths" (Prov. 3:5-6).

Who is wise enough to give counsel to God (Rom. 11:34)? Who knows enough to tell God what is fair and right? It is not our place to question and doubt. It is our place to believe and do. We must first realize who God is and who we are.

One must be careful not to let his emotions become his standard of authority. It is possible for one to be satisfied with a belief and practice and yet be lost (Matt. 7:21-23; 2 Thess. 2:10-12).

3. Brethren. There seem to be a few who think that, if they can find some preacher who says their situation is all right, their marriage must be right. If brother _____ says it's true, it's true. Some judge the validity of a position by the number of brethren who agree or disagree. This approach makes the brethren the standard rather than the Bible. Brethren are humans. They can be wrong, and many times are. God warned about following the multitude to do evil (Exod. 23:2). Jesus said that few would be in the narrow way while many would be in the broad way that leads to destruction (Matt. 7:13-14).

Perhaps the reason that some appeal to brethren as their standard is that they love the praises of men more than the praises of God (John 12:42-43). Our goal should be to be "accepted of him" (2 Cor. 5:9).

The *word of God* is the only standard of authority that pleases God. There must be some objective standard. One recognizes this principle in other areas of life. He has no problem seeing that, if one didn't have a standard, there would be chaos. There has to be some common standard that we all can look to in order to determine what is right and wrong.

The Bible is that standard. Peter said, "If any man speak, let him speak as the oracles of God" (1 Pet. 4:11). Paul wrote, "And whatsoever ye do in word or deed, do all the name of the Lord Jesus, giving thanks to God and the Father by him" (Col. 3:17).

If one has *faith*, he will accept what the Bible teaches because the *Lord* said it, not because it fits a preconceived idea, for it may not; not because it is what we have always believed, because it may not be; not because he likes the consequences, for he may not. What the word

NOTES

of God says about divorce and remarriage may not be easy to accept. Sometimes it is bitter (Rev. 10:9).

4. Various Positions. Below we have a brief summary of the numerous positions of brethren that will be examined in this book.

1. Death is the only cause for remarriage. This position states that there can be no divorce and remarriage at all for any reason. One can only remarry if his mate is dead.

2. Divorce and remarriage for any cause. The idea is that one can get a divorce for any reason and is thus free to remarry.

3. Divorce and remarriage for any legal cause. As long as the divorce is legal (according to civil law) then it is all right. With the "no fault divorce" of today, there isn't much difference in this position and the previous one.

4. Guilty party free to remarry. This is a very popular position that states that the one who is put away for fornication is free to remarry.

5. The believer who is forsaken by an unbelieving mate is free to remarry. If a Christian is married to a non-Christian, this position says that the Christian is not and never has been bound to his or her mate. If there is a divorce (for any cause) the believer is free to remarry.

6. Aliens are not subject to God's law on marriage. This position and the previous one are practically the same. This one states that non-Christians are not subject to the law found in Matthew 19:9.

7. Divorces and remarriages are all washed away at baptism without separation. The idea is that one who has been divorced and remarried for unscriptural reasons can be baptized and continue living with that unscriptural mate. Baptism makes that unscriptural marriage scriptural. No separation is required.

8. Mental divorce. This concept is that one who is put away for unscriptural causes can remain married in his mind to his first mate until he/she remarries. Then he/she puts her/him away "in his mind" for adultery and is now free to remarry.

9. Divorce and remarriage are scriptural for the innocent party who has put away his or her mate for fornication. This is the teaching of Matthew 19:9. This is the position that this writer takes.

NOTES

Questions

Verses to remember: "Now therefore make confession unto the Lord God of your fathers, and do his pleasure: and separate yourselves from the people of the land, and from the strange wives. Then all the congregation answered and said with a loud voice, As thou hast said, so must we do" (Ezra 10:11-12).

Discussion

1. Why do the people of God need to study these issues?_____

2. What kind of problems are churches having over divorce and remarriage?_____

3. Why is the subject so controversial?_____

4. Discuss how people use family situations and emotions as standards not only in divorce and remarriage, but also in other issues._____

5. Discuss some examples of God's requirements that may not seem fair and right or may not make sense to us. Give some that are not given in this lesson._____

True or False

_____ 1. Questions must never be asked when divorcees obey the gospel or place membership.

_____ 2. God has never required any married people to separate.

_____ 3. The Bible teaching on divorce and remarriage is very difficult to understand.

_____ 4. Some of God's laws are unfair.

_____ 5. Our only standard is the word of God.

Find the Passage

1. "Trust in the Lord with all thine heart; and lean not unto thine own understanding." _____

2. "O Lord, I know that the way of man is not in himself: it is not in man that walketh to direct his steps." _____

3. "There is a way that seemeth right unto a man, but the end thereof are the ways of death."_____

4. "Ye have transgressed, and have taken strange wives, to increase the trespass of Israel. Now therefore make confession unto the Lord God of your fathers, and do his pleasure: and separate yourselves from the people of the Land, and from the strange wives." _____

5. "And whatsoever ye do in word or deed, do all in the name of the Lord Jesus, giving thanks to God and the Father by him." _____

Answer in a Few Words

1. What do divorce statistics tell us? _____

2. What causes for divorce were discussed in this lesson? _____

3. What makes the issue of divorce and remarriage difficult? _____

4. Name three false standards of authority to which brethren sometimes appeal. _____

5. If some well known preacher says that a certain divorcee can remarry, shall we automatically conclude that he is right? _____

Multiple Choice

_____ 1. If we have *faith,* we will accept the Bible teaching because (a) we like the consequences, (b) the Lord said it, (c) it fits our preconceived ideas.

_____ 2. If we have a family member who unscripturally divorces and remarries we should (a) believe the Bible and reprove the person, (b) change our position on divorce and remarriage, (c) look for a preacher who will approve.

_____ 3. If we learn from the Bible that certain people can never marry again or must separate we should (a) reject the teaching saying "That's unfair," (b) become angry with the preacher who teaches that, (c) learn to accept the truth.

_____ 4. Our responsibility is to (a) question and doubt God's law, (b) determine what is fair and sensible, (c) believe and do God's law.

_____ 5. The scriptural cause for divorce is (a) irreconcilable differences, (b) fornication, (c) incompatibility.

Fill in the Blank

1. The New Testament teaching on divorce and remarriage is _____ to understand.

2. The issue of divorce and remarriage is difficult to resolve because of _____ and situations with _____ _____ that cry out for some _____ answer from the Word of God to justify that human element.

3. Since family situations _____ , then if we use them as standards of authority what would be right for one would be wrong for another.

4. Our whole goal in life should be to be "_____ _____ _____."

5. What _____ right and fair to us may not be what is _____ and _____ in the sight of _____.

Lesson 2

Understanding Marriage and Other Important Terms

A verse to remember: *"When a man hath taken a wife, and married her, and it come to pass that she find no favour in his eyes, because he hath found some uncleanness in her: then let him write her a bill of divorcement, and give it in her hand, and send her out of his house"* (Deut. 24:1).

Confusion is created when people who speak of divorce and remarriage use terms in different ways. One person may use the term "marriage" to mean one thing while someone else uses it to mean another. Somebody may use the term "adultery" to describe one thing while another uses it in a different way.

Much of the controversy over divorce and remarriage will be resolved if we correctly understand some definitions. In fact, divorce would be prevented if we would simply learn and accept God's plan for marriage.

God's Plan for Marriage (Gen. 2:18-25)

After creating Adam, God saw that man's loneliness was not good (v. 18). Adam looked over all the animals and beasts and found no helper suited to him. So, God took woman from the side of man making her a helper that is suitable for his needs.

Let's focus our attention for a moment on verse 24. There are a couple of basic lessons found in this verse.

1. Permanence in marriage. This is clearly seen in the reference that Jesus made to this text. The Pharisees came to Jesus asking, "Is it lawful for a man to put away his wife for every cause?" In contrast to that, Jesus responded, "Have ye not read, that he which made them at the beginning made them male and female, and said, For this cause shall a man leave father and mother, and shall cleave to his wife: and they twain shall be one flesh?" (Matt. 19:4-5). Notice that Jesus contrasted the concept of ending marriage for any cause to the quotation of Genesis 2:24. Also, the Pharisees understood his affirmation of permanence for they asked why Moses gave divorcement.

2. Commitment in marriage. One who chooses to marry must "cleave unto" his mate. The word translated "cleave" in Matthew 19:5 means "to join fast together, to glue, cement" (W.E. Vine, *Expository Dictionary of New Testament Words* I:196). Marriage is entered by free choice which should cause one to be committed to prove his choice is right. The permanence which God requires is the basis for the commitment.

Sexual union is an important part of marriage. The two being "one flesh" involves cohabitation, though it includes more. Marriage is honorable and the bed undefiled (Heb. 13:4).

What Constitutes Marriage?

Marriage is "a compact (covenant, DVR) entered into by a man and a woman, to live together as husband and wife" (*Funk & Wagnalls Standard Dictionary* 781).

The Bible doesn't directly address the question of "what constitutes marriage?" However, a few points can be established to determine what makes a marriage.

1. Intention to live together. The act of leaving father and mother and cleaving to one's mate indicates an agreement to be married (Matt. 19:5-6). Obviously, no one has ever married who did not intend to be married. Mary, the mother of Jesus, was "espoused" to Joseph, which indicates an agreement they had to be married (Matt. 1:18). Malachi 2:14 speaks of the "wife of thy covenant."

2. Compliance with society or the laws of the land. Since the Bible doesn't tell us specifically what constitutes marriage, we must go to the laws of society to determine what constitutes a public ratification of the marriage. God requires that one be obedient to the laws of the land (Rom. 13:1-7). Thus, whatever the law requires for marriage, God requires for marriage as long as God's law is not violated (Acts 5:29). Jesus talked with a woman who had been married five times and then was living with a man without meeting the requirements of society or law. She said, "I have no husband," and Jesus said, "He whom thou hast now is not thy husband" (John 4:16-18).

Deuteronomy 24 tells us that a "writing of divorcement" was necessary to end a marriage. If some legal process is necessary to end the marriage, we conclude that there must be some similar process necessary to begin the marriage. The marriage feast that Jesus attended (John 2:1-11) and spoke of in a parable (Matt. 22:1-14) illustrates that the point at which people are married is not left to their own whims or a mental state, rather it was when certain requirements were met.

3. Cohabitation? Is it necessary to engage in sexual intercourse before a couple is scripturally married? That question has been debated when our inquiry of "What constitutes marriage?" is made. I believe the Bible answer is "no." The sexual act is a blessing that comes as a result of marriage. In fact, God has regulated that cohabitation take place within marriage (Heb. 13:4). If a couple is not married before the first sex act, what right do they have to engage in it? Consequently, they would have to commit fornication in order to get married. Consider that Joseph took Mary as his wife before he knew her sexually (Matt. 1:24-25).

Marriage Is Marriage

These requirements apply to God-approved and God-disapproved marriages. When the requirements are met, the couple is married. Whether God approves of the marriage or not, it is still a marriage. In Mark 6:17-18 we see that God didn't approve of Herod's marriage and yet the text says they were "married." Some brethren want to talk about people who are married "in the eyes of God" and refer to those in adultery as not "really being married." However, in the New Testament, whether God approved or disapproved, the couple was considered married. Jesus said that the man who puts away his wife and *marries* another commits *adultery*. Does he have a right? No! Does God approve? Absolutely not! It's adultery. But, Jesus said he was married. Consider other passages like: Matthew 5:32; Mark 10:11-12; Luke 16:18; Romans 7:2-3.

Arguments That Sexual Union Constitutes Marriage

Believe it or not, there are those who believe that, if a man and woman engage in intercourse, marriage has been constituted. Arguments are made from 1 Corinthians 6 and Genesis 2.

1. 1 Corinthians 6:16-17. It is argued that the man who is joined (sexually) to an harlot is then married to her for the text says the two are "one body." We have already noticed that sexual union isn't necessary to constitute marriage, but is a blessing that comes because people are married. The text under question doesn't say that this man married the harlot. The apostle is showing that he has brought his body (which is the temple of God) and joined it with the harlot's body which makes his body unfit as the temple of God.

The fornicator apparently thought that the sex act was simply a physical performance that didn't affect their personalities. But, he was wrong. The sex act unites the personalities of the partners. The two become one. Their personalities merge. Thus, the man who is supposed to be a Christian becomes more and more like the harlot.

"Joined" refers to being closely united with another (cf. Luke 10:11; 15:15; Acts 5:13; 8:29; 9:26; 10:28). The word itself doesn't necessarily refer to sexual union or marriage. In 1 Corinthians 6:16 the word translated "joined" is in the middle voice (meaning man joins himself to the harlot) whereas the word translated "joined" in Matthew 19:6, which does refer to marriage, is in the active voice (meaning God does the joining of man and wife). Thus the man joined to an harlot is not married to her.

In Exodus 22:16-17 a man who would lay with a virgin was not married at that point for her father had an option to let her marry (cf. Gen. 34:24).

If sexual union constitutes marriage, would the man who had cohabited with four women be married to all of them?

2. Genesis 2:24. This passage is taken by some to mean that the first sex act constitutes marriage for it says that the couple would be "one flesh." Look again at the context of Genesis 2. There was not an helper suited for Adam. So, God took a rib from Adam and made woman. The flesh that once was one person is now two. These two become one flesh by being united in marriage. The flesh that was once one person, then divided, is united again in marriage. It includes sexual union, but involves much more.

Therefore, this does not constitute a euphemism for sexual relations. It constitutes a unity of the totality of man and woman. The two were husband and wife (one) before the sexual union. Though the marriage of man and woman includes sexual relations, the idea of the "one flesh" includes far more than this. It includes the psychological, emotional, social, and spiritual as well as the physical aspects of the union of a man and woman, making them husband and wife (Gary L. Headrick in *Marriage, Divorce and Remarriage* by Maurice W. Lusk, III:157).

Before there can be marriage, there has to be some agreement. If the sex act within itself constitutes marriage, then every sex act constitutes a marriage. That would mean every rape and illicit relationship would make a marriage because those acts make the two "one" in some sense.

Terms Defined

1. Divorce. The word translated "divorce" or "put away" simply means "to loose from, sever by loosening, undo ... to set free" (Joseph Henry Thayer, *Greek-English Lexicon* 66). Divorce is the legal ending or severing of a marriage (cf. Deut. 24:1; Isa. 50:1; Jer. 3:8). Whether we call it "divorce," "putting away," or "annulment," the ending of the marriage is divorce.

As in the case of marriage, divorce is divorce. Whether God approves or disapproves it is still divorce. The man who puts away his wife unscripturally is divorced. Jesus said he has put her away (Matt. 5:32; 19:9). Thus, just because a divorce is legal (in harmony with civil law) doesn't mean that it is scriptural. Divorce does not mean that the parties automatically have a right to remarry (1 Cor. 7:10-11; Matt. 19:9).

2. Fornication. This term is a broader one than adultery. Walter Bauer defines the word translated "fornication" as "prostitution, unchastity, fornication, of every kind of unlawful intercourse" (*A Greek-English Lexicon of the New Testament and Other Early Christian Literature* 693). Thayer says, "prop. of illicit sexual intercourse in general" (532). This definition would include homosexuality, lesbianism, and incest. However, it does not include a man who looks upon a woman to lust (Matt. 5:28). Though the text says he has committed adultery in his heart, the Lord uses "adultery" to emphasize where lust leads. To illustrate, in 1 John 3:15 the man who hates his brother is called a "murderer." Yet, the sin is hatred and not murder. The term "murderer" is used to emphasize where hatred leads. In both cases, the text shows the end result of the evil thought (cf. Maurice W. Lusk, III, *Marriage, Divorce and Remarriage* 41).

Generally the word "fornication" refers to unlawful intercourse of the unmarried (e.g. to avoid fornication one is to marry — 1 Cor. 7:2-5). However, the term is also applied to illicit sexual conduct of married people (1 Cor. 5:1; Rev. 2:20).

3. Adultery. The term translated "adultery" in Matthew 19:9 means "to have unlawful intercourse with another's wife" (Thayer 417). The noun "adulterer" "denotes one who has unlawful intercourse with the spouse of another..." (*Vine's*, I: 33). Adultery is a more specific term than fornication. It generally refers to sexual activity between a married man and a woman not his wife or between a married woman and a man not her husband. As the terms are generally used, fornication is the broader term that includes adultery. Whereas adultery describes only a part of what is included in fornication.

Sometimes the words are used interchangeably (Rev. 2:20-22). Occasionally the term fornication will be used to describe what would generally be called adultery (1 Cor. 5:1).

As the term is used in Matthew 19:9 it refers to an illicit relationship between those who are unscripturally married. Adultery can be committed (as is in Matt. 19:9) with one's own wife. Paul said that the woman who *marries* another would be called an *adulteress* (Rom. 7:2-3).

Some have argued that adultery simply means "covenant breaking" thus contending that a couple guilty of adultery can repent of the covenant breaking and continue in that marriage. Would that definition and application apply to passages which speak of spiritual adultery (Jer. 3:8, 9; Ezek. 23:37; Hos. 4:13)? Would those guilty simply have to say "I'm sorry" and then continue in their sin? In Matthew 5:28 is one fantasizing covenant breaking? The Jews brought to Jesus a woman who was taken in the very act of adultery (John 8:8), which tells us that there is more involved in adultery than covenant breaking. In Matthew 5:32 the put away one (who is not guilty of covenant breaking) commits adultery when she remarries.

It is argued by some that only the first sexual act is adultery. That severs the bond which makes one free to continue in that marriage after he repents of the sin. To the contrary, the New Testament shows that a couple commits adultery every time they cohabit, from the first act to the last. The word translated "committeth adultery" in Matthew 19:9 is in the *present* tense in the Greek. In the Greek the *time* of action is secondary; the *kind* of action is what is primarily denoted. The present tense tells us that the adultery is continuous action. Leonard Latkovsky, Professor of Classical Languages, Bellarmine College, Louisville, Kentucky comments, "And the present tense form of the Greek form *moichatai* = commits adultery means 'continuous action at any time', i.e. as long as the condition of the second marriage continues to exist" (written statement to Gene Frost).

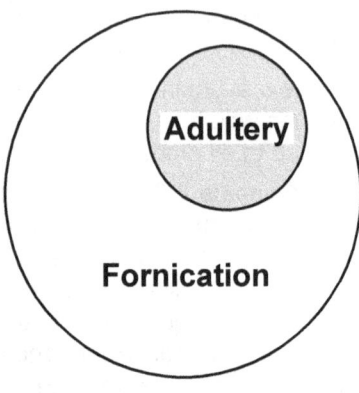

Paul wrote to the Colossians and mentioned "fornication" among a number of sins. Then, he states that they had "lived in them" (Col. 3:5, 7). So, one can *live in* adultery, which shows that it involves more than a one time act. The woman who marries another while her first husband lives would be called an "adulteress" (Rom. 7:2-3). To say the least, she remains in adultery as long as he is living. Again, continuous action is described.

4. Separation. This refers to a husband and wife not living together though they are still married. It is not the same as a divorce. I only know of one passage which refers to separation (without divorce) and that is 1 Corinthians 7:5.

5. Bond. The bond is a covenant with God that joins us to our mate. God is the one who joins (bonds or yokes together), thus only God can loose. One who is scripturally married is "bound by the law to" his mate (Rom. 7:2). In context with verse 3, it is that bond (with the first mate) that makes the second marriage adulterous. It is clear from Romans 7:2-3 that the marriage and the bond are not the same. It is possible to be married to one while bound to another. This bond obligates one to leave and cleave (Matt. 19:5) and restrains from sexual relations with another (Rom. 7:1-4).

NOTES

Questions

A verse to remember: "Let every soul be subject unto the higher powers. For there is no power but of God: the powers that be are ordained of God" (Rom. 13:1).

Discussion

1. Discuss the confusion that is created by using terms like "marriage," "adultery," and "divorce" in different ways. _____
   _____

2. Discuss the contrast in Matthew 19:3-9 that shows the permanence of marriage. _____
   _____

3. Discuss how permanence in marriage is the basis for commitment. _____
   _____

4. Discuss the meaning of "one flesh." _____
   _____

5. Discuss the difference in divorce and separation. _____
   _____

True or False

_____ 1. All those who are married are bound to their mates.

_____ 2. Fornication does not include homosexuality, lesbianism, and incest.

_____ 3. An unscriptural marriage is still a marriage.

_____ 4. "One flesh" includes more than the sexual act.

_____ 5. Cohabitation is a requirement to get married.

Find the Passage

1. "Mortify therefore your members which are upon the earth; fornication, uncleanness ... In the which ye also walked some time, when ye lived in them:" _____

2. "Whosoever putteth away his wife, and marrieth another, committeth adultery: and whosoever marrieth her that is put away from her husband committeth adultery." _____

3. "Then Joseph being raised from sleep did as the angel of the Lord had bidden him, and took unto him his wife: And knew her not till she had brought forth her firstborn son...." _____

4. "What? Know ye not that he which is joined to an harlot is one body? For two, saith he, shall be one flesh." _____

5. "For Herod himself had sent forth and laid hold upon John, and bound him in prison for Herodias' sake, his brother Phillip's wife: for he had married her. For John had said unto Herod, It is not lawful for thee to have thy brother's wife." _____

Answer in a Few Words

1. What does "fornication" mean? _____
2. What does "adultery" mean? _____
3. What is the difference in "adultery" and "fornication"? _____
4. What does "divorce" mean? _____
5. What does "bond" or "bound" refer to? _____
6. What does "separation" mean? _____
7. What is the difference between "divorce" and "separation"? _____

Multiple Choice

_____ 1. When a man and woman unscripturally marry, they are (a) not really married in the eyes of God, (b) really married, though God disapproves, (c) not in agreement with civil requirements for marriage.

_____ 2. A woman who puts away her husband, meeting civil requirements, is (a) only separated, (b) not really divorced in the eyes of God, (c) divorced, though God may approve or disapprove.

_____ 3. The expression "one flesh" (a) refers only to sexual intercourse, (b) does not include sexual intercourse, (c) includes the psychological, emotional, social, and spiritual, as well as the physical, aspects of the union of a man and woman.

_____ 4. A couple who unscripturally marry (a) commit adultery only the first time they cohabit, (b) commit adultery every time they cohabit, (c) can repent and continue in that marriage.

_____ 5. 1 Corinthians 6:17 teaches that a Christian who cohabits with an harlot (a) is married to her, (b) has made his body unfit as the temple of God.

_____ 6. Those unscripturally married are (a) bound to each other, for all of those who are married are bound, (b) not bound to each other, for at least one mate is bound to another.

Fill in the Blank

1. The _____ in marriage is the basis for _____.
2. _____ to live together and compliance with _____ or the _____ of the land are requirements for marriage.
3. Jesus said that the man who puts away his wife and _____ another commits _____.
4. Divorce does not mean that the parties _____ have the right to _____.
5. _____ is the general term that refers to unlawful intercourse, while _____ is the specific term.
6. Colossians 3:5, 7 show that those unscripturally married "_____ _____" adultery.

Lesson 3

Matthew 19:9 (1)

A verse to remember: *"And I say unto you, Whosoever shall put away his wife, except it be for fornication, and shall marry another, committeth adultery: and whoso marrieth her which is put away doth commit adultery"* (Matt. 19:9).

When the issue of divorce and remarriage is discussed, one verse immediately comes to mind, that being Matthew 19:9. If any passage needs to be properly understood in a study of this type, Matthew 19:9 is the text. Though other points and passages must come into view, this verse bears the main burden. Our purpose in this and the next lesson is to learn what this text says.

Historical Background

Jesus's discussion with the Pharisees takes place in the dominion of Herod Antipas who had John the Baptist beheaded for telling him that his marriage to Herodias was unlawful (Mark 6:16-28). Though there is no indication in the text, possibly the Pharisees thought the same would happen to Christ were he to say the same things in Herod's jurisdiction.

There were two major schools of thought on the causes of divorce. Apparently, a heated debate continued among the Jews over the interpretation of Deuteronomy 24:1-4. At the head of the discussions were Rabbis Shammai and Hillel who were heads of rabbinical schools in Jerusalem about a century before Christ.

Both schools taught that divorce was lawful. The question concerned the cause or grounds for divorce. *Rabbi Shammai* contended that divorce is lawful only for adultery or some sexual sin. His contention is more biblical only in so far as Moses didn't approve of divorce for every cause. *Rabbi Hillel* affirmed that divorce is lawful for every cause (e.g. even to over salting or ill-cooking the food). This was the more popular idea. Divorce for every cause was widely practiced, especially around Jerusalem. There was also a third school led by *Rabbi Akiba* which was quite similar to Hillel, but said that divorce was lawful even if a man found a woman more pleasing.

The Context

Our study of verse 9 will be enhanced when we have a good knowledge of the context (vv. 3-12).

1. The Pharisee's question (v. 3). The Pharisees came to Jesus and asked, "Is it lawful for a man to put away his wife for every cause?" They were attempting to put him in conflict with either or both of the rabbinic schools. It may be that they wanted to turn those who held to the popular idea against him. Obviously, they were not asking their question out of a desire to know the truth.

The question seemed to center around Deuteronomy 24:1-4, for verse 7 indicates that it was on their mind. The very wording of their question tells us that Hillel's interpretation was in their thoughts.

2. Jesus answers by pointing to God's law at the beginning (vv. 4-6). Jesus did not directly address the issue centering around Deuteronomy 24:1-4. Rather, he indicts them of ignorance of God's original law on marriage by saying, "Have ye not read...?"

The Lord does not set one passage against another (e.g. Gen. 2:24 vs. Deut. 24:1-4) as we shall see later. Rather, he points beyond customs, rabbis, traditions, and even Moses to the beginning (Gen. 1:27; 2:24). By pointing to the beginning, Jesus gives four reasons why one can't put away his mate for every cause.

a. God created one man for one woman (Gen. 1:27). No spare mates were created just in case the first marriage didn't work. God never said, "If this marriage doesn't work, try someone else."

b. Mates must cleave to each other (Gen. 2:24). To "cleave" means "to join fast together, to glue, cement" (W.E. Vine, *Expository Dictionary of New Testament Words* I:196). God intended for a man to cleave to his wife (and vice versa) and it be a permanent situation. That is the way it was at the beginning; the way it should have been then and the way it ought to be till the world ends. This is why it is wrong to put away one's mate for every cause. Genesis 2:24 should determine a man's attitude toward his wife and putting her away and not Deuteronomy 24.

c. A man and his wife are one flesh (Gen. 2:24). One is the only number that can't be divided (at least as it refers to people). "One" suggests total possession of each other. The two are one in mind, spirit, goals, direction, emotions, feelings, and will. Matthew Henry said, "A man's children are pieces of himself, but his wife is himself" (5, 214).

d. God has joined man and woman together in marriage. The word translated "joined" (used only here and in Mark 10:9) means "to fasten in one yoke, yoke together" (Thayer 594). When God has bound them together, man has no right to put his mate away for any cause.

3. The Pharisees ask about Moses and the bill of divorcement (vv. 7-8). Now they attempt to put Christ in conflict with Moses. By citing Deuteronomy 24:1-4, they think this is just another way to discredit Jesus since reverence for Moses was second only to God. However, they had perverted Moses by speaking of divorcement as a command.

Casuistic Law

IF ... (vv. 1-3) — *Protasis*

- Put her away for "uncleanness"
- She becomes another man's wife
- The second man puts her away or dies

THEN ... (v. 4) — *Apodosis*

- May not remarry her first husband

2

What does Deuteronomy 24:1-4 actually say? Moses was dealing with conditions that were bound to occur. Nothing is said to encourage divorce and remarriage. This text simply prohibits the remarriage of the put away woman to her first husband. Nothing is said about God's approval of the divorce and her remarriage to the second man. "In these verses, however, divorce is not established as a right; all that is done is, that in case of a divorce a reunion with the divorced wife is forbidden" (Keil and Delitzsch, *The Pentateuch* III:417).

This is a case of "casuistic law." The contruction is "If ... Then...." The "if" clause is called the "protasis" and the "then" clause the "apodosis." Casuistic law does not command or approve of the protasis, but states that when those things happen *then* (the apodosis) here is what the law says must be done. For example, if you borrowed my car I might say, "If you have a wreck, then you must call the police." I did not tell you to have a wreck, nor suggest that I would approve of such. I only said that *if* that happens, you *then* must call the police. Exodus 21:10 is a passage with this type of construction. "If he take him another wife" does not command or approve of polygamy. Rather, if he does take another wife, he then is not to diminish her food, raiment, and duty of marriage. Also consider verses 18-20. Another example would be laws regulating the punishment for murder, which obviously do not endorse it.

The NKJV and NASV clarify this point. The KJV seems to indicate that God approves of a man putting away his wife for uncleanness and her remarriage to the second man by saying "then *let him* write her a bill ... she *may go* and be another man's wife" (Deut. 24:1-2, emphasis mine, DVR). However, the NKJV simply states it as a thing the man does, rather than saying he may do it. It reads: "and he writes her a certificate ... and goes and becomes another man's wife." The NASV says, "and he writes her a certificate ... and goes and becomes another man's wife." Neither translation indicates that God approves of the man putting away his wife or her remarrying the second man.

> The careful reader will notice that the renderings of the AV and RV differ materially. AV reads in the second part of ver. 1: *"then let him* write a bill," etc., RV has "*that he shall* write"; etc., while the Heb. original has neither "then" nor "that; but the simple conjunction "and": There is certainly no command in the words of Moses, but, on the other hand, a clear purpose to render the proceeding more difficult in the case of the husband" (*ISBE* II:863).

Deuteronomy 24:1-3 constitute the protasis, simply stating that the man puts away his wife and she remarries another man and he puts her away or dies. This is stated without comment about God's approval. Then verse 4 constitutes the apodosis, stating what can or cannot be done in the event that the things previously mentioned take place.

The fact that God did not approve of a man putting away his wife for "uncleanness" and her remarriage to the second man is seen in that she was "held to be defiled by her second marriage" (*Pulpit Commentary,* 3: 381). This defilement indicates that her second marriage was not approved of God. Jeremiah 3:1, which makes reference back to Deuteronomy 24, compares the woman who married the second man to an harlot. Many commentators have suggested that she was defiled only with reference to her first husband and that she was justified in her second marriage. However, I ask why would she be defiled to him and only to him if her second marriage was approved of God?

What was the purpose of such laws as Deuteronomy 24:1-4? It was to discourage frivolous divorces (for every cause) which was common among the Jews. If he was going to put her away, he had to give her a certificate or bill of divorce (a legal transaction). He could not just throw her out. Thus, this law protected the wife (e.g. from later accusations of fornication). He might have been made to think twice about the divorce in that reconciliation was forbidden. The real purpose of the denial of reconciliation was to prevent this couple from polluting the land (cf. Jer. 3:1).

What is the meaning of "uncleanness"? I do not think that anyone really knows what all is and isn't included in this term. It is not all that important to know. Remember that the text is not saying that God approves of divorce for the cause of "uncleanness," but simply says if he puts her away for that cause. We can safely say that it does not refer to (1) adultery or fornication for that was punishable by death (Deut. 22). (2) Neither was it suspicion of adultery, for Numbers 5 dealt with a test for that. (3) It was not evidence that she was not a virgin, for again Deuteronomy 22:13-21 gives a test for that. *Young's Concordance* defines it as "a thing offensive" (1012). The same word translated "uncleanness" is used in Genesis 42:9, 12 with reference to flaws in the land. Thus, I believe it simply refers to some flaw that her husband may find in her character (cf. Hastings *Dictionary of the Bible,* III: 275).

There is a practical lesson from Deuteronomy 24. Today a lot is said about the poor innocent party who couldn't help being put away. Surely God wouldn't punish him by not allowing him to remarry. Yet, the woman of Deuteronomy 24 was in a similar situation (though not parallel in all

NOTES

respects). Though she could not help being put away, she could not remarry her first husband.

Jesus said that Moses "suffered" them to put away their wives (Matt. 19:8). Divorce was already a common practice in Israel long before Moses wrote Deuteronomy 24. "Suffered" means "to permit, allow, give leave" (*Thayer* 245). God (and Moses) tolerated divorce for every cause even though he did not approve, for Jesus said "from the beginning it was not so." Also, God hates putting away (Mal. 2:16). Throughout the Old Testament God tolerated many things which he didn't approve (e.g. polygamy).

Whether Jesus refers to Deuteronomy 24 as the text that tolerated divorce or to another statement by Moses (that may not be recorded), I do not know. I know that from the beginning it was not so. Though tolerated, the practice of divorce for every cause was contrary to Genesis 1 and 2. The last phrase of verse 8 is present perfect which suggests that it was "not so" in the past and is "not so" in the present.

4. Jesus teaches his law (v. 9). Jesus said, "And I say unto you,..." Despite their practices, Moses's toleration, and rabbinical interpretation, this is his law. To put away one's mate for every cause and remarry results in adultery. Since fornication is a violation of the principle of Genesis 2:24, the Lord allows divorce for that cause. The meaning and application of this verse will be dealt with in more detail in the next lesson.

5. The Disciples' Response (vv. 10-12). Having moved into the house, the disciples continue the discussion with interest (Mark 10:10). They said that, if a man can't put away his wife for any and every cause (do with her as he pleased), he would be better off not to marry. Bauer translates part of verse 10, "If the relationship of a man with his wife is like this" (*A Greek-English Lexicon of the New Testament* 26). They had made the "attractiveness of marriage contingent upon the possibility of easy divorce" (David Hill, *Matthew,* 281).

The disciples introduced the question about celibacy (v. 10). The Lord then picks up on that statement and says, "All men cannot receive this saying, save they to whom it is given" (v. 11). "This saying" refers to their statement "it is not good to marry" (v. 10). Jesus points out that such a statement would not apply to every person, but it would to some. He gives three cases where that would be true. (1) Those who are born eunuchs (physically incapable of sexual relations) are better off living single. (2) Those who have been made eunuchs (by the cruelty of men) are not fitted

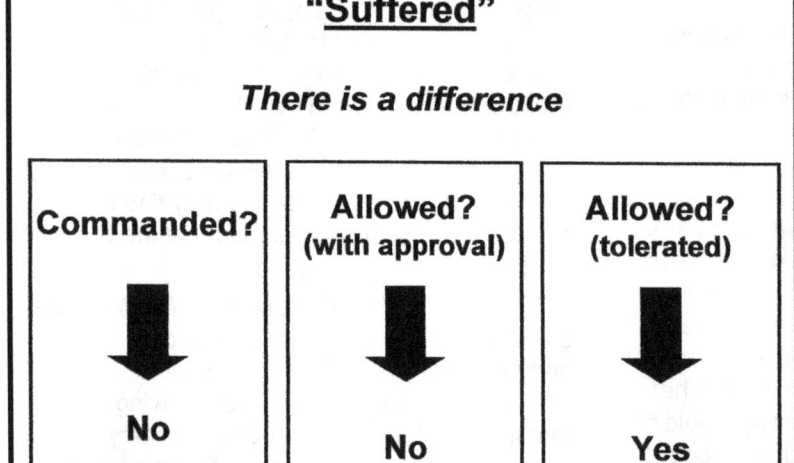

for marriage. (3) Add to that those who become eunuchs for the sake of the kingdom of God. This third class might also include some who have no right to remarry.

Is It of the Old or New Covenant?

It is argued that Matthew 19:9 is not binding today for it is a part of the old covenant. The contention is that Jesus was explaining the Old Testament law on divorce and remarriage. Since the exception clause found in Matthew 5:32 and 19:9 is not repeated after Pentecost, we are told that it is not a portion of the law of Christ.

1. We will reject more than Matthew 19:9. If Matthew 5:32 and 19:9 are no part of the New Testament, than neither is the whole book of Matthew. If that be true, then we must also reject Mark, Luke, and John. It is interesting to note that all of the gospels were written after Pentecost.

2. Contrast in Matthew 5 and 19 to the Law of Moses. In both texts Jesus puts his teaching in contrast to the law of Moses. In Matthew 5 he would begin by saying, "Ye have heard that it was said by them of old time . . ." and then in contrast he would say, "But I say unto you: . . ." This is done at least six times in this chapter (vv. 21-22, 27-28, 31-32, 33-34, 38-39, 43-44). While it is true that Jesus deals in part with rabbinical interpretation in this chapter, there are definite contrasts to the law of Moses.

The Pharisees saw a contrast in the teaching of Christ and that of Moses (Matt. 19:7). They said Moses had "commanded" to give a writing of divorcement. Jesus more correctly said that Moses "suffered" it. However, there is still a contrast, for he said, "And *I say* unto you..." (v. 9, emphasis mine, DVR).

3. Jesus' teaching applies now. A law can be stated before it comes into effect (e.g., Mark 16:16). Since Jesus had and has all authority, the disciples were to teach those whom they baptized "to observe all things whatsoever" he "commanded" them (Matt. 28:18-20).

The law and prophets were taught until John, but since then the kingdom of heaven was preached (Luke 16:16). Just two verses later is a parallel verse to Matthew 19:9 (Luke 16:18).

If we are to believe that Matthew 19:9 is no part of the New Testament because it was spoken before Pentecost, I wonder about a number of other passages. I wonder about Matthew 18:17; John 3:5; Matthew 7:21; John 14:6; Luke 22:30; Matthew 28:18-20 and Matthew 13 (the parables of the kingdom); are these explanations of the law of Moses? Do they apply today? Take such passages as Matthew 5:28, if it is not applicable today, then when did it apply? It certainly was not a part of the Old Law.

4. If not applicable now, it never was. If Matthew 19:9 does not apply today, it never did apply. It certainly was not a part of the law of the Old Testament. Under that law, the fornicator was put to death (Deut. 22), thus there was no need to put her away. It could not apply to the future, for in heaven there is no marriage (Matt. 22:30). Thus, we would have a meaningless passage.

Just because those writers after Pentecost never mentioned the exception (for fornication) does not mean that Matthew 19:9 is not binding, any more so than the fact that Jesus did not mention death as a cause for remarriage would mean that Romans 7:1-4 does not apply.

Textual Problems

Please bear with the remainder of the lesson as we deal with some technical matters about our text.

NOTES

1. The Exception Phrase. Some have argued that the phrase "except it be for fornication" doesn't belong in our text, but that it was added by some scribe. However, there is no textual evidence to reject it. I wrote to F.W. Gingrich and Bruce M. Metzger (both are well known Greek scholars) and asked them, "Is there any textual evidence to reject the phrase 'except it be for fornication'?" Both men answered "*no*."

This phrase is supported by Matthew 5:32. In fact the real question among scholars has been the variant readings concerning the wording of this phrase. Should it be worded as it appears in Matthew 19:9 or as it is worded in Matthew 5:32?

There is no available manuscript that omits it. The Majority text, Westcott-Hort text, and the Nestle text all include this phrase.

2. The remarriage clause (v. 9b). The statement "and whoso marrieth her which is put away doth commit adultery" is questioned and even omitted in the NASV, NIV, and RSV because the Sinaitic manuscript (one of the oldest) omits it. Though missing in such manuscripts as *Aleph* (Sinaitic), *D* (fifth-sixth century), *L* (eighth century) and *C* (fifth century, corrected by at least three readers), it is contained in such manuscripts as P^{25} (fourth century), *B* (Vaticanus), and the original copy of *C*. In fact, the majority of the manuscripts contain it. Thus, the evidence for it is greater than against it.

It is retained in the Majority text and in such translations as the KJV, ASV, and the NKJV. The 267 scholars behind these three versions saw fit to include it in their works. I asked Bruce M. Metzger, "Is there any textual evidence to reject the phrase 'and whoso marrieth her which is put away doth commit adultery'?" His answer was "no." *Pulpit Commentary* says, "It has very high authority in its favor" (15:245).

It is thought that since the Siniatic manuscript is so old, it should carry more weight than the many that retain it. First, let us consider that Matthew 1-24, part of John and 2 Corinthians are also missing from that manuscript. If we reject Matthew 19:9b, are we ready to reject Mark 16:9-20 which is also not found in that manuscript? Secondly, "making textual decisions on the basis of how three or four 'old' uncials read should be abandoned because they do not give a complete picture of the second century traditions" (Harry A. Sturz, *The Byzantine Text-Type and New Testament Textual Criticism* 65). When all is said and done, the phrase is still found in Matthew 5:32 and Luke 16:18.

Questions

A verse to remember: "Therefore shall a man leave his father and mother, and shall cleave unto his wife: and they shall be one flesh" (Gen. 2:24).

Discussion

1. What significance would the fact that the discussion of Matthew 19:3-12 was taking place in the dominion of Herod Antipas possibly have? _____

   _____

2. Discuss the differences in the conservative and liberal thoughts of Shammai and Hillel. Which had the greater following? Discuss how the more liberal ideas on divorce and remarriage always have a greater following. _____

   _____

   _____

3. Discuss the purpose of such laws as Deuteronomy 24:1-4. _____

   _____

   _____

4. What are the consequences of rejecting the exception phrase and the remarriage clause? _____

   _____

   _____

5. Discuss the consequences of saying that Matthew 19:9 is a part of Old Testament law. _____

   _____

   _____

6. Discuss the practical lesson we learn from Deuteronomy 24:1-4. _____

   _____

True or False

_____ 1. The NASV and NKJV better translated Deuteronomy 24:1-4.

_____ 2. Moses allowed (approved) of divorce for uncleanness.

_____ 3. Jesus agreed with Shammai's interpretation of Deuteronomy 24:1-4.

_____ 4. Several manuscripts omit the exception phrase in Matthew 19:9.

_____ 5. God allowed divorce for any cause in the Old Testament, though he did not approve it.

Find the Passage

1. "They say, If a man put away his wife, and she go from him, and become another man's, shall he return unto her again? Shall not that land be greatly polluted? but thou has played the harlot with many lovers; yet return again to me, saith the Lord." _____

2. "So God created man in his own image, in the image of God created he him; male and female created he them." _____

3. "When a man hath taken a wife, ... because he hath found some uncleanness in her: then let him write her a bill of divorcement .... she may go and be another man's wife .... if the latter husband ... write her a bill of divorcement .... or if the latter husband die .... Her former husband .... may not take her again to be his wife...." _____

4. "The law and the prophets were until John: since that time the kingdom of God is preached, and every man presseth into it." _____

5. "Teaching them to observe all things whatsoever I have commanded you...." _____

Answer in a Few Words

1. What was Shammai's teaching on divorce? What was Hillel's? _____

2. What does "cleave" mean? _____

3. How does Genesis 1:27 fit into the discussion of divorce for every cause? _____

4. In what sense are man and wife considered "one"? _____

5. What is casuistic law? _____

6. What is the meaning of "uncleanness" (Deut. 24:1)? _____

7. In what sense did Moses allow divorce for every cause? _____

Multiple Choice

_____ 1. The exception phrase is mentioned (a) in all of the Gospels, (b) only by Jesus and Paul, (c) only in Matthew's record.

_____ 2. The remarriage clause (Matt. 19:9b) is found (a) only in this verse, (b) also in Mark 10:11-12, (c) also in Matthew 5:32 and Luke 16:18.

_____ 3. The disciples thought that the teaching of Christ was (a) not strict enough, (b) too strict, (c) in agreement with the practices of the day.

_____ 4. Jesus said that Moses (a) commanded, (b) allowed (only tolerated), (c) allowed (with approval) divorce among the Jews.

_____ 5. The teaching of Christ is (a) an explanation of the Old Testament, (b) not binding unless repeated after Pentecost, (c) binding today.

Fill in the Blank

1. Such manuscripts as _____, _____, _____ and _____ omit the remarriage clause (Matt. 19:9b), while such manuscripts as _____, _____, and _____ retain it.

2. Such scholars as _____ and _____ say there is no textual evidence to reject the exception phrase.

3. Jesus said that the saying "it is good not to marry" applied to _____, _____, and _____.

4. Jesus said that even though Moses _____ men to put away their wives, "_____ _____ _____ it was not so."

5. The "if" clause of casuistic law is called the _____ and the "then" clause is called the _____.

6. Rabbi _____ said a man can put away his wife if he found a woman more pleasing.

7. The term "uncleanness" cannot refer to _____ or the _____ of adultery or evidence that she was not a _____.

Lesson 4

Matthew 19:9 (2)

A verse to remember: *"But I say unto you, That whosoever shall put away his wife, saving for the cause of fornication, causeth her to commit adultery: and whosoever shall marry her that is divorced committeth adultery"* (Matt. 5:32).

John Murray said that Matthew 19:9 is "the most pivotal passage in the New Testament on divorce." Thus, we need to properly understand and apply it. Our text is not all that hard to understand. Martin Luther said, "Matthew 19:9 is a blunt, clear, plain text." The problem comes when the text does not agree with one's life.

The Exception Phrase

Why is Matthew the only writer to include the exception phrase (Matt. 5:32; 19:9)? If each Gospel had all the details of the other three, there wouldn't be a need for all four. Each writer may tell something different (not contradictory). For example, Matthew 1 tells of the announcement of the birth of Christ to Joseph, while Luke 1 tells of the announcement to Mary. Also the accounts of the great commission differ a little. Matthew records Jesus saying "teaching them to observe all things...," whereas Mark and Luke say nothing about that. Luke includes repentance, whereas Matthew and Mark do not. Compare Matthew 28, Mark 16, and Luke 24. This illustrates why we need all of the Bible. The same is true regarding the subject of marriage.

One possible explanation is that in Matthew 19 the question being discussed was concerning putting away for "every cause." Thus, in teaching his law, Jesus shows that there is one cause (fornication) and only one. Mark's account doesn't address the matter from the standpoint of "every cause."

Other writers (Mark, Luke, and Paul) deal with the blanket rule, only Matthew mentions the exception. Several different people may try to explain to a foreigner about a red light. Most would probably say, "All vehicles must stop at a red light." However, one may tell him, "All vehicles, except emergency vehicles, must stop at a red light."

Why did Jesus allow divorce for fornication (v. 9) when he said, "from the beginning it was not so" (v. 8)? Again the question was concerning divorce for "every cause" (v. 3). Moses tolerated divorce for "every cause" (v. 8). That was the thing that was not so from the beginning. However, when he says, *"And I say unto you..."* (v. 9, emphasis mine, DVR) he is stating what his law is now. That law allows divorce for fornication.

Does the exception phrase modify the last clause, "and whoso marrieth her which is put away doth commit adultery"? It is argued that there is an "ellipsis" in the last clause of the text. An "ellipsis" is an omission of a word or words that are necessary to complete a sentence. Thus, we are told that, to properly understand this clause, we must supply the exception.

However, as Matthew 19:9 reads, it is not grammatically incomplete. No word or words must be supplied (grammatically or reasonably) to make sense.

The exception phrase cannot grammatically modify both the first and last parts of Matthew 19:9. As it modifies the first clause it is an *adverbial* phrase (qualifying "shall put away"). Yet, if it modified the second clause it would be an *adjectival* phrase (qualifying "is put away"). This cannot be done grammatically! I wrote to Bruce M. Metzger asking him, "Does the exception clause ('except it be for fornication') modify the phrase 'and whoso marrieth her which is put away doth commit adultery'?" His answer was "no, it qualifies the preceding clause."

The following quotes, compiled by Gene Frost, are from teachers and professors of English and Greek who say that this phrase cannot modify both clauses.

> In Matt. 19:9 the original Greek text translated "except for fornication" modifies the "putting away" on the part of the man and does not modify the person who is put away. And the present tense form of the Greek form *moichatai* = commits adultery means "continuous action at any time", i.e. as long as the condition of second

marriage continues to exist adultery continues to exist (Leonard Latkovski, Professor of Classic Languages, Bellarmine College, Louisville, Kentucky).

In my opinion, the phrase, "except it be for fornication," applies to the first clause but not to the last" (Dr. Harry Sturz, Greek Department, Biola College, La Mirada, California).

The modifying clause (except it be for fornication) applies *only* to the first person mentioned, in the first half of the sentence. It does not apply, grammatically or syntactically, to the person ("whoso marrieth her who is put away") in the second half of the sentence (Donald A. Drury, M. A., English Department, Long Beach City College).

There is no evidence from the English, Greek, this text, or any other that demands that this exception modify the last clause.

The consequence of having "except for fornication" apply to the person who is put away is that the fornicator would be protected. The put away fornicator would be free to remarry while one put away for burning the bread could not. A little fornication would make the second marriage all right. Who can believe such?

Parallel Passages

1. Matthew 19:9. "And I say unto you, Whosoever shall put away his wife, except it be for fornication, and shall marry another, committeth adultery: and whoso marrieth her which is put away doth commit adultery."

The emphasis in this passage is on the sin of unjustly putting away one's mate for "every cause." This text includes the exception phrase and the remarriage (concerning the put away one) clause.

2. Matthew 5:32. "But I say unto you, That whosoever shall put away his wife, saving for the cause of fornication, causeth her to commit adultery: and whosoever shall marry her that is divorced committeth adultery."

Jesus begins with "But I say unto you," which shows a contrast to the old law as well as the rabbinical interpretation of it.

Emphasis in this text is on the man causing his wife to commit adultery by unjustly putting her away. This text is the only one that says he causes her to so sin. "First the statement that divorce will cause the woman to become an adulteress is simply another way of condemning the second union she will most probably be obliged to contract in her situation" (William A. Heth and Gordon J. Wenham, *Jesus and Divorce,* 14). "Far better, it would seem to me, is therefore the translation, 'Whoever divorces his wife except on the basis of infidelity exposes her to adultery; or something similar'" (William Hendriksen, *New Testament Commentary: Matthew,* 306). This adultery is not committed until she remarries. He simply puts her in a position where she will either remain single or commit adultery. Statistics show that most divorced people remarry.

This text includes the exception phrase and the remarriage (concerning the put away one) clause.

3. Mark 10:11-12. "And he saith unto them, Whosoever shall put away his wife, and marry another, committeth adultery against her. And if a woman shall put away her husband, and be married to another, she committeth adultery." Mark's account simply states the blanket rule. There is no exception phrase or remarriage (concerning the put away one) clause.

Jesus said that the man who puts away his wife and remarries commits adultery "against her." It is "against her" (most likely the second wife) because they (he and his first wife) are still bound, though not married (Rom. 7:2-3). The bond will be discussed in more detail in Lesson 5.

In verse 12 Jesus turns the matter around and applies it to the woman who would put away her husband. Mark is the only writer that records this. The wife putting away her husband was rare among the Jews (in fact, the law made no provision for it). Yet, it was quite common among the Gentiles to whom Mark writes. Matthew wrote to the Jews.

4. Luke 16:18. "Whosoever putteth away his wife, and marrieth another, committeth adultery: and whosoever marrieth her that is put away from her husband committeth adultery." As Mark, Luke merely states the blanket rule, leaving out the exception. However, this text does have the remarriage (concerning the put away one) clause. On the surface it seems that verse 18 doesn't fit the context. Yet, the whole chapter convicts the Pharisees of loose attitudes toward the law. "Then the Lord illustrated the abiding nature of the law in a point where the Pharisees notoriously transgressed it" (*Lutheran Commentary*, IV: 306-307). In verse 16 the Lord introduces the gospel of the kingdom. Then just two verses later Jesus speaks his law on divorce and remarriage.

Reasons To "Put Away"

Personal Dislike	Jesus Allowed Only One (Matt. 19:9)
Burns the Bread	
Cannot Get Along	⬇ Fornication

Application of Our Text

We now come to the heart of Lessons 3 and 4 by seeing what the text really says. How is it to be applied?

1. Divorce. Jesus does not command or require divorce, but it is permitted with approval. There are many reasons why one might obtain a divorce (incompatibility, personal dislike, burning the bread, irreconcilable differences and even fornication). However, Jesus allowed only one cause: fornication, whether there will be any remarriage or not.

2. Remarriage. In the case of remarriage after divorce, the general rule is that it is adultery. The one exception is when one puts away his or her mate for fornication. Carefully consider the charts 5 and 6 (next page).

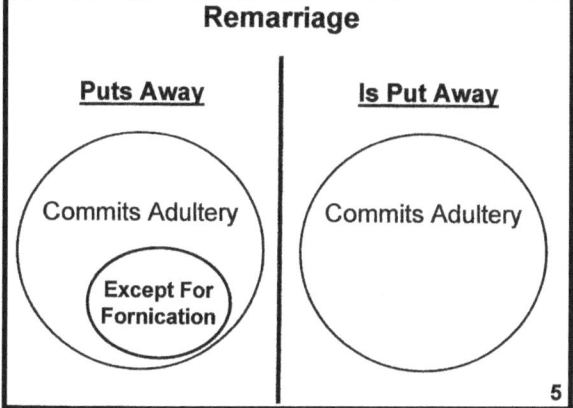

If the one who puts away remarries, it is adultery if the divorce was for some cause other than fornication. It is not adultery if the divorce was for fornication. If the put away one remarries, it is adultery whatever the cause, fornication or not.

Matthew 19:9 contains two complete clauses joined by "and": The one who puts away (exception: fornication) and remarries commits

Matthew 19:9

Part A

"And I say unto you, Whosoever shall put away his wife, except it be for fornication, and shall marry another, committeth adultery . . ."

> Puts Away — (Fornication) — **Remarries** — No Adultery
> Puts Away — (No fornication) — **Remarries** — Adultery

Part B

". . . and whoso marrieth her which is put away doth commit adultery."

> Is Put Away — Remarries — Adultery

6

Marrying The "Put Away" One

"Whoso marrieth her which is...

Put Away {
 Personal Dislike
 Burns The Bread
 Cannot Get Along
 Fornication
}

...doth commit adultery."

7

adultery *and* when the one who is put away remarries, he commits adultery.

Obviously, when the put away one (whether for fornication or another reason) remarries, it is adultery.

When no fornication is involved, remarriage for both partners is adultery. It does not matter which remarries first, both remarriages are adultery. Consider charts 8 and 9 (see top of page 35).

God does not allow any divorce in which both parties are free to remarry.

Order of the Text

Some have attempted to justify practically all remarriages when fornication is committed, whether before or after the divorce. For example, if Jack puts away Jill for burning the bread and later he commits fornication, it is argued that she is now free to remarry. The order of events here would be (1) Put away, (2) Fornication, (3) Remarriage. Or if Jack puts away Jill for burning the bread and she then remarries, it is thought by some that any fornication Jack may then commit would justify Jill's second marriage. The order of events here would be (1) Put away, (2) Remarriage, (3) Fornication.

The order of events that Jesus gave in our text is (1) Fornication, (2) Put Away, (3) Remarriage. To change that order is just as wrong as to tamper with the order of events in Mark 16:16. Consider chart number 10 (page 35).

The above perversions of Matthew 19:9 would demand that the word "and" in the clause "and whoso marrieth her that is put away...." mean "or." Thus, it would be Jack committing adultery if he remarries first, *or* Jill committing adultery if she remarries first. Yet, "and" is translated from *kai* which does not mean "or." I wrote to both Metzger and Gingrich and asked if *kai* could possibly be "or." Metzger said, "no"; Gingrich said, "'or' is not likely." In addition to that, the translators used the word "and" not "or."

NOTES

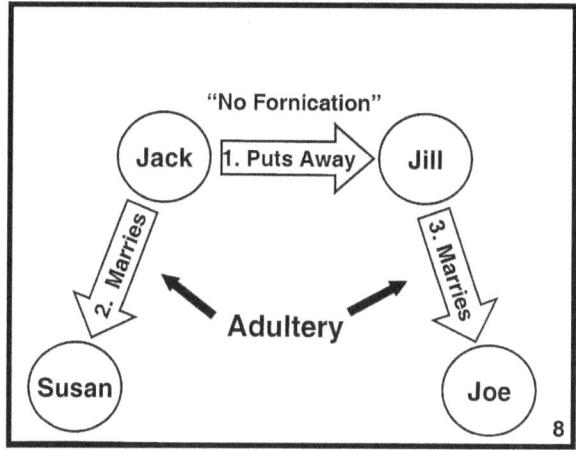
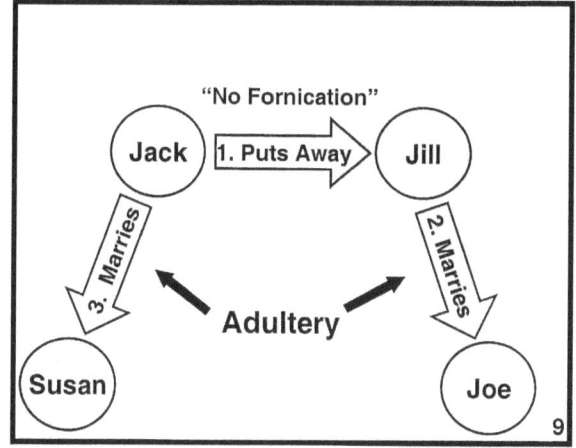

God's Order -vs- Man's Order

	Mark 16:16	
1. Believe	2. Baptized	3. Saved
	MAN:	
1. Believe	2. Saved	3. Baptized

	Matt. 19:9	
1. Fornication	2. Put Away	3. Remarriage
	MAN:	
1. Put Away	2. Remarriage	3. Fornication
1. Put Away	2. Fornication	3. Remarriage

Questions

Verses to remember: "And he saith unto them, Whosoever shall put away his wife, and marry another, committeth adultery against her. And if a woman shall put away her husband, and be married to another, she committeth adultery" (Mark 10:11-12).

Discussion

1. Talk about how each gospel contains something different. _____
   _____
   _____

2. Discuss some possible explanations for Matthew being the only writer to include the exception phrase. _____
   _____

3. Discuss how Luke 16:18 fits into its context. _____
   _____
   _____

4. Discuss the consequences of saying that "except it be for fornication" modifies "and whoso marrieth her which is put away." _____
   _____

5. Who has the right to remarry after divorce. _____
   _____

True or False

_____ 1. Matthew 19:9 includes the exception phrase and remarriage (for the put away one) clause.

_____ 2. Luke 16:18 contains the exception phrase.

_____ 3. The phrase "except it be for fornication" modifies both clauses in Matthew 19:9.

_____ 4. There is an ellipsis in the last clause of Matthew 19:9.

_____ 5. The Greek word *kai* means "and" and not "or."

Find the Passage

1. "And he saith unto them, Whosoever shall put away his wife, and marry another, committeth adultery against her. And if a woman shall put away her husband, and be married to another, she committeth adultery." _____

2. "Whosoever putteth away his wife, and marrieth another, committeth adultery: and whosoever marrieth her that is put away from her husband committeth adultery." _____

3. "And I say unto you, Whosoever shall put away his wife, except it be for fornication, and shall marry another, committeth adultery: and whoso marrieth her which is put away doth commit adultery."

4. "But I say unto you, That whosoever shall put away his wife, saving for the cause of fornication, causeth her to commit adultery: and whosoever shall marry her that is divorced committeth adultery." _____

5. "He that believeth and is baptized shall be saved; but he that believeth not shall be damned."
_____

Answer in a Few Words

1. What is meant by "causeth her to commit adultery"? _____

2. Why does Mark 10:12 mention the woman putting away her husband, when Matthew doesn't?
_____

3. What is the order of the events in Matthew 19:9?_____

4. If Jack puts away Jill for burning the bread and he then remarries, does she commit adultery if she remarries?_____

5. Does God allow divorce for any cause when there is no intention of remarriage? _____

Multiple Choice

_____ 1. The remarriage clause (for the put away one) is found (a) only in Matthew19:9, (b) in Mark 10:11-12, (c) in Matthew 5:32, 19:9, and Luke 16:18.

_____ 2. The man who puts away his wife and remarries commits adultery against her (the second wife) because (a) they (he and his first wife) are still married, (b) they (he and his first wife) are still bound, (c) she (the first wife) protested the divorce.

_____ 3. The order of the events in Matthew 19:9 is (a) put away, fornication and remarriage, (b) put away, remarriage, and fornication, (c) fornication, put away, and remarriage.

_____ 4. The exception phrase (a) cannot, (b) does, (c) may, modify the last clause, "and whoso marrieth her which is put away...."

_____ 5. The man who puts away his wife "causeth her to commit adultery" because (a) she has no guilt in her remarriage, (b) he forced her to remarry, (c) he places her in a situation where if she does remarry it is adultery.

Fill in the Blank

1. As the exception phrase modifies the first clause it is used as an _____ phrase. If it modified the second clause it would be used as an _____ phrase.

2. John Murray said that _____ is the most _____ passage on the subject of _____.

3. _____ and _____ are the only two passages that include the exception phrase.

4. Matthew writes to the _____ while Mark writes to the _____

5. Martin Luther said that Matthew 19:9 is a _____, _____, _____ text.

Lesson 5

Who Can Marry? The Difference in the Marriage and the Bond

Verses to remember: *"For the woman which hath an husband is bound by the law to her husband so long as he liveth; but if the husband be dead, she is loosed from the law of her husband. So then if, while her husband liveth, she be married to another man, she shall be called an adulteress: but if her husband be dead, she is free from that law; so that she is no adulteress, though she be married to another man"* (Rom. 7:2-3).

This lesson discusses two different things, which, if properly understood, will clear up many questions that are raised. When I first began to study these issues, I called two well known gospel preachers and asked them some questions. One said that he thought it best to summarize the New Testament teaching by listing those who are given a right to marry. The other said that if one could establish a clear distinction between the *marriage* and the *bond,* he would be able to answer most of the questions and arguments raised. I have since found that both men were right.

Who Can Marry?

By this question we simply refer to those who have a scriptural right to marry. We must find a passage that so authorizes these people to marry. If one desires to marry or remarry and does not qualify as one who is given the right, then such a marriage would be adulterous.

1. One who has never been married. God intended that man should leave his father and mother and cleave unto his wife (Matt. 19:4-5). Paul said that marriage is honorable (Heb. 13:4). The same writer said, "But if they cannot contain, let them marry: for it is better to marry than to burn.... But and if thou marry, thou hast not sinned; and if a virgin marry, she hath not sinned" (1 Cor. 7:9, 28).

2. One whose mate is dead. Paul argued, "But if her husband be dead, she is free from that law; so that she is no adulteress, though she be married to another man" (Rom. 7:3).

3. One who puts away his/her mate for fornication. Jesus said, "Whosoever shall put away his wife, except it be for fornication, and shall marry another, committeth adultery...." (Matt. 19:9). It is argued by some that this verse teaches that one can divorce for fornication, but he cannot remarry. Most of the "church fathers" argued this position, e.g., Origen, Tertullian, Clement of Alexandria, Irenaeus, Justin Martyr, *et. al.* However, when we look again at Matthew 19:9 it is obvious that, if the man who puts away his wife *for a cause other than fornication* and remarries *commits adultery*, then the man who puts away his wife for fornication and remarries *does not commit adultery.*

4. Those reconciling. After urging the couple not to divorce, Paul said that if they do, "let her remain unmarried, or be reconciled to her husband..." (1 Cor. 7:11). They have a right to remarry each other. That does not suggest that they necessarily have a right to remarry someone else.

While one party may have the right to marry or remarry, the one whom he/she is marrying must also have a right or that marriage will be adulterous. If Jack has a right to marry and Jill (whom he is marrying) does not have a right, both will be guilty of adultery (Matt. 19:9).

Authority and the *silence of the Scriptures* must be respected. We must abide within the "doctrine of Christ" or we have not God (2 John 9). Paul urges that we do all things "in the name of Jesus Christ" (i.e., by his authority, Col. 3:17). In all things we must be able to put our finger on the passage for what we believe and practice.

Who Can Marry?

1. **One who has never been married**
   (Matt. 19:4,5; Heb. 13:4; 1 Cor. 7:9, 28)

2. **One whose mate is dead**
   (Rom. 7:3)

3. **One who puts away his mate for fornication**
   (Matt. 19:9)

4. **Those reconciling**
   (1 Cor. 7:11)

11

And when God is silent, we are not to take that as permission to act and speak. Rather, the silence of God is non-permissive. Christ could not be a priest on earth for he sprang out of Judah, "of which tribe Moses *spake nothing* concerning priesthood" (Heb. 7:14, emphasis mine, DVR). The very reason I oppose instrumental music and the missionary society is that concerning these things God "spake nothing"! That is the very same reason that I oppose anyone else other than those mentioned above getting married; God "spake nothing" about it! We must be careful that we not allow our emotions and human reasoning to justify things that cannot be found in the word of God.

The Difference in the *Marriage* and the *Bond*

1. Confusion. When we fail to make a distinction between the marriage and the bond, our terminology becomes quite confusing. I hear people talking about the "marriage bond" indicating that "marriage" and "bond" are the same. The idea then is that, when they are no longer married, they are no longer bound. A lot is said today about being married "in the eyes of men" and married "in the eyes of God." The same is true of divorce (e.g. divorced "in the eyes of men" and "divorced in the eyes of God"). Thus, to these people one could be married "in the eyes of men" but not married "in the eyes of God." A distinction is made between marriage (or divorce) that is "real" and "legal." If God approves, we are told that it is "real"; but if God does not approve, it is not "real'; but only married or divorced "accommodatively." Thus, to them there is no such thing as an unscriptural marriage, for if it is unscriptural, it is not really a marriage. Confused? I warned you.

2. There is a difference. This is obvious from the fact that in Romans 7:2, 3 the woman is *bound* to her first husband even though she is *married* to her second husband.

Marriage is a relationship entered into by agreement and ratified by compliance with civil law. The *bond* is a covenant with God that joins one to his mate. When a couple scripturally marry, God "joins" (i.e., yokes) them together (Matt. 19:6). This takes place in the mind of God. God does the joining and only God can do the loosing. In a scriptural marriage there is a covenant that involves three (God, husband, and wife, Mal. 2:14). The "law of her husband" (Rom. 7:2) refers to the bond or the "law which binds the wife to her husband" (G. Kittel, *Theological Dictionary of the New Testament* IV:1070). God binds those who are scripturally married (Rom. 7:2; 1 Cor. 7:39).

Notice that we are *bound* "by the law" *to* our mate. I believe that the law that binds us is God's law of one mate for life (Gen.1:27; 2:24).

3. It is possible to be bound to one and married to another. Again, that was the case in Romans 7:2, 3. This woman is "bound by the law to her husband" even though she is "married to another man." That is what makes the second marriage adultery.

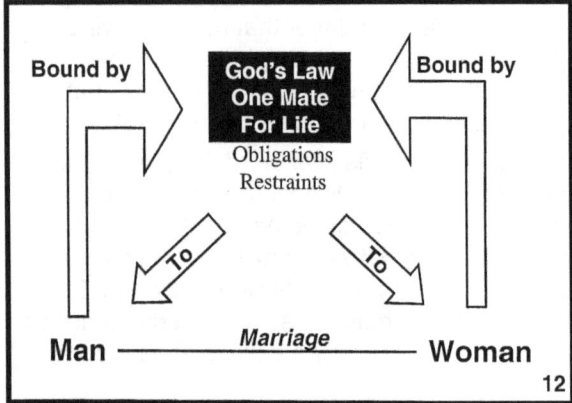

It is possible for one to be released from the yoke and the other party not. When Jack married Jill, God yoked (joined) them together (Matt. 19:6). However, when Jack put Jill away for fornication, God released him from the yoke, while Jill is still yoked (bound, Matt. 19:9). See Chart 14.

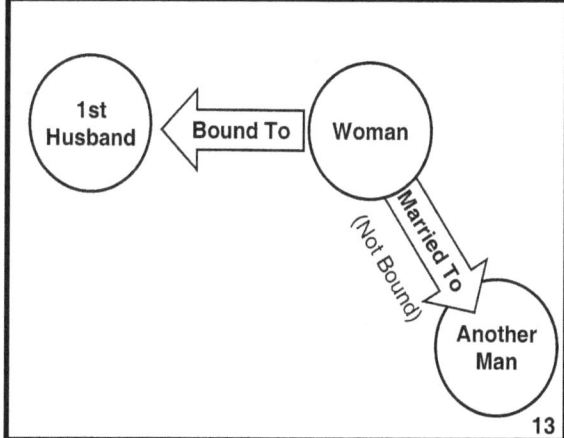

4. Thus Marriage Is Marriage and Divorce Is Divorce.

We need to be careful of talking about marriage that is marriage and marriage that is not marriage, and in the same light, of divorce that is divorce and divorce that is not divorce. In this we are engaging in ambiguity and playing semantical gymnastics. A person who is married may not be said to be unmarried, and a person unmarried may not be said to be married. We may use adjectives to modify or qualify our terms, but we may not change the meaning of our terms to make them lose their essential identity. If we try to play this game, language loses its function (Maurice W. Lusk, III, *Marriage, Divorce and Remarriage,* 96-97).

A marriage may or may not have scriptural authority but it is a marriage nonetheless; and those involved in the marriage may not be said to be "not married" (*Ibid.,* 98).

If the marriage is scriptural and approved of God, it is a marriage. If the marriage is unscriptural and not approved of God, it is still a marriage. Let's consider some cases in the Bible where the marriage was unscriptural (thus adultery) and yet God still said that it was a *marriage* (really). Herod "had married" Herodias (Mark. 6:17). However, John told him that it was unlawful for him to have her. Nevertheless, God said he had *married* her. In Matthew 19:9 we read that a man who puts away his wife and marries another commits *adultery*. Scriptural? No! Married? Yes. Then in Romans 7:3 the woman is called an *adulteress* because she is *married* to another man.

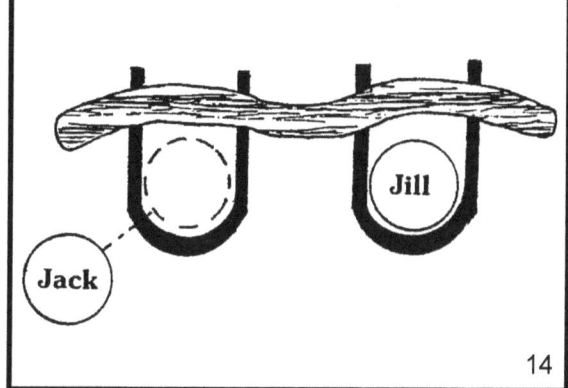

Remember, that in the text Jesus only used the term "marries" *one* time. Thus, if he meant "really married" then *both* of the above men are really married, whether God approved or not. If Jesus meant that they were not really married, but only "in the eyes of men"; then *both* of the above men are married "only in the eyes of men." The same is true of "put away" (divorce) in both cases. We can't have it both ways in this text! See Chart 17.

If we begin to let married mean unmarried, believer mean unbeliever, in the covenant mean out of the covenant, where will it all end? (Jerry Gross, *Marriage, Divorce and Remarriage* by Martin W. Lusk, III, 166).

5. Four positions one can be in with reference to being bound. (1) One can be bound and scripturally married (Matt. 19:5-6; Rom. 7:2). (2) One can be bound and unmarried (1 Cor. 7:10-11). (3) One mate can be bound and unmarried while the other mate is free to remarry (Matt. 19:9). (4) One mate can be bound to his first mate while unscripturally married to another (Mark 6:17-18; Rom. 7:2-3).

6. Loosing. This is a thing that God does since he does the joining (Matt.

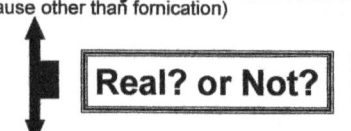

Is It Real Or Not?

"And I say unto you, Whosoever shall put away his wife, except it be for fornication, and shall marry another, committeth adultery: and whoso marrieth her which is put away doth commit adultery."

Man - "Puts Away" Wife - "Marries Another" - Adultery
(for cause other than fornication)

Real? or Not?

Man - "Puts Away" Wife - "Marries Another" - No
(for fornication)   Adultery

19:6). Divorce does not necessarily loose one. As we have seen from Romans 7:2-3 it is even possible to marry another and be bound to the first mate.

Loose means to set at liberty, free to remarry (Rom. 7:2-3). Who is loosed? (1) One whose mate has died (Rom. 7:2-3). (2) One who has put away his/her mate for fornication (Matt. 19:9).

7. Arguments answered. We must consider a couple of arguments that are made in an attempt to prove that there is marriage that is real and marriage that is only in the "eyes of men."

a. 1 Corinthians 7:11: This passage tells a woman who is *unmarried* to be reconciled to her *husband*. The argument is that she was both unmarried and married (unmarried in the eyes of men and married to her first mate in the eyes of God). However, the word "husband" is translated from the Greek *anēr* which is simply the word for "man." Thus, this woman is to be reconciled to the man to whom she is bound.

b. Mark 6:17-18: This passage tells us that Herod was *married* to Philip's *wife*. The argument is that she was married (really) to Philip, but

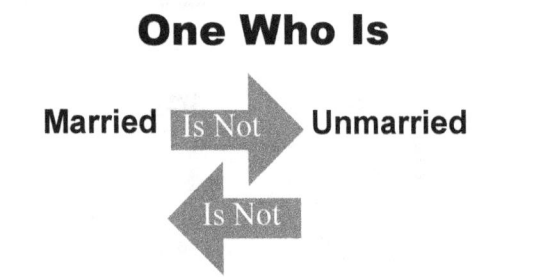

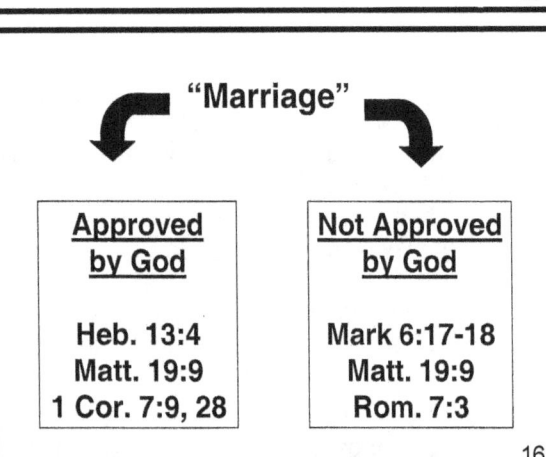

only in the "eyes of men" to Herod. The word "wife" is translated from the Greek *gunē* which is simply the word for "woman." Philip was the man to whom Herodias was bound. The terms "husband" and "wife" do not always refer to one who is presently married (Rom. 7:2-3; Luke 20:28). Both passages prove the very point we have been making in this lesson.

NOTES

Questions

Verses to remember: "And he answered and said unto them, Have ye not read, that he which made them at the beginning made them male and female, And said, For this cause shall a man leave father and mother, and shall cleave to his wife; and they twain shall be one flesh? Wherefore they are no more twain, but one flesh. What therefore God hath joined together, let not man put asunder" (Matt. 19:4-6).

Discussion

1. Discuss the position held by the "church fathers." Why did they believe as they did? _____

2. Discuss whether any and every divorcee has a right to remarry. _____

3. Discuss the seriousness of respecting the silence of the Scriptures. _____

4. Discuss the confusion caused when we equate the marriage with the bond, and talk about marriage "in the eyes of God" (that is real) and marriage "in the eyes of men" (that is not real)._____

5. Discuss the significance that the distinction between the marriage and bond has on the overall discussion of divorce and remarriage. _____

True or False

_____ 1. One who is divorced cannot remarry his/her first mate.

_____ 2. There is a difference in marriage (and divorce) that is "real" and that which is "legal."

_____ 3. Since God does the joining, only he can do the loosing.

_____ 4. It is possible to be bound to one and married to another.

_____ 5. All who marry or remarry are bound.

Find The Passage

1. "For the woman which hath an husband is bound by the law to her husband so long as he liveth...." _____

2. "For it is evident that our Lord sprang out of Juda; of which tribe Moses spake nothing concerning priesthood." _____

3. "If a man's brother die, having a wife ... his brother shall take his wife...." _____

4. "For Herod himself had sent forth and laid hold upon John, and bound him in prison for Herodias' sake, his brother Philip's wife: for he had married her. For John had said unto Herod, It is not lawful for thee to have thy brother's wife." _____

5. Give three passages where God calls an adulterous union a "marriage." _____

Multiple Choice

_____ 1. If God does not approve of a marriage (a) it is not real, (b) it is marriage only in the "eyes of men," (c) it is still a marriage.

_____ 2. If one is married he (a) cannot be bound to another, (b) can be bound to another.

_____ 3. One whose mate is dead (a) is bound to that mate, (b) is loosed from that mate, (c) must remain unmarried.

_____ 4. The law that binds one to his mate is (a) one mate for life (Gen. 1:27; 2:24), (b) no divorce except for fornication (Matt. 19:9), (c) a prohibition to return to one's first mate (Deut. 24:1-4).

_____ 5. The "joining" (Matt. 19:6) refers to (a) marriage, (b) the bond, (c) only the legal paperwork.

Fill in the Blank

1. _____ , _____ , _____ and _____ are those who are authorized to marry.

2. If Jack has a right to marry and Jill (whom he is marrying) does not have the right, both will be guilty of _____.

3. Romans 7:2-3 shows a woman who was _____ _____ the law to her husband, while she was _____ to _____ man.

4. God does the joining (Matt. 19:6), thus _____ _____ can do the loosing.

5. It is possible to be _____ to _____ while _____ to _____.

6. One who is married is not _____ and one who is unmarried is not _____.

Lesson 6

Death Only Cause for Remarriage

A verse to remember: *"And I say unto you, Whosoever shall put away his wife, except it be for fornication, and shall marry another, committeth adultery: and whoso marrieth her which is put away doth commit adultery"* (Matt. 19:9).

With this lesson we begin analyzing some of the errors that brethren advocate on the subject of divorce and remarriage. While most of the errors taught on divorce and remarriage are to the left (granting rights to divorce and remarry where God has not given the right), there are some who are to the extreme right (denying the right of divorce and remarriage to those that God has given a right).

Maybe this extreme right comes from some who are motivated because of the loose attitudes that are so prevalent. If so, we agree with the motive and are likewise opposed to the liberal thought. However, the solution to the problem is not to take the other extreme. We cannot agree with the conclusions that these brethren have reached.

The Position Stated

This position states that only death severs the bond. It says that there is no scriptural ground for divorce and remarriage. Even divorce for fornication is not scriptural and remarriage is not allowed.

We are told that Matthew 5:32 and Matthew 19:9 are not applicable today. These are thought to be explanations of the law of Moses or possibly some kind of alteration of that law for the Jews then living. Since the exception found in these two texts is not mentioned after Pentecost, it is thought that it does not apply today.

This basic concept comes in more than one form. Some teach that there is no scriptural ground for divorce and remarriage. They condemn all divorces and all remarriages (except in the case of death). Others teach that divorce for fornication is allowed, but they condemn all remarriages.

Divorce and Remarriage Permitted for Fornication

God put Israel away for fornication. Israel's relationship with God is described as a marriage. Thus, when Israel went after other gods it was called fornication (Ezek. 16:26). God then put Israel away for fornication (Jer. 3:6, 8). For God to metaphorically speak of his dealing with Israel as marriage and then divorce for fornication tells me that divorce for fornication is not out of harmony with God's law on marriage from the beginning.

Jesus taught it. (1) Matthew 5:32. The contrast throughout this chapter shows that what Jesus taught is not a part of Moses's law. This verse begins with "but I say unto you" which indicates a contrast to verse 31. (For more see Lesson 3, Section III.) While the general rule is that one who puts away and remarries commits adultery, Jesus gave one exception: fornication. (2) Matthew 19:9. This passage is part of the new covenant for Jesus taught the gospel of the kingdom (Matt. 4:23; 13:19-ff; 18:3). When the apostles went forth preaching (which things we are told are binding today), they simply proclaimed what Jesus commanded them (Matt. 28:19). If our text does not apply now, I wonder about other passages, like John 3:5; Matthew 18:17; 7:21; Luke 22:30 and Mark 16:16. Are these applicable today?

If Matthew 19:9 is not true now, then we must say that it never was true, for we are told that divorce for fornication is contrary to the law at the beginning. Thus, it could not be true then or now. Another interesting matter is why the advocates of this position want to apply Matthew 19:3-6, but tell us that verse 9 does not apply. For more see Lesson 3.

Again, as in Matthew 5:32, we have the general rule (one who puts away and remarries commits adultery) with one exception added: fornication. What would the passage mean if the phrase "except it be for fornication" were not in it? It would mean that all divorces and remarriages would be wrong. The advocates of the position under examination would then tell us that it is binding. Now, what does it mean with the exception phrase added? It means the same as Luke 16:18 and Mark 10:11-12 (which we are told are binding), with one simple exception added to the blanket rule.

Arguments Answered

1. "In Matthew 5:32 and 19:9 Jesus was giving an explanation of the law of Moses (Deut. 22 and 24)."

Let's suppose that Matthew 5:32 and 19:9 do state exactly what Deuteronomy 22 and 24 say, what does that have to do with whether they apply today? We also wonder if other passages in Matthew 5 which have the same construction as verses 31-32 are explanations of the old law (vv. 21-22, 27-28, 33-34, 38-39, 43-44). What Jesus taught in Matthew 19:9 was in harmony with God's law at the beginning (vv. 4-5). He showed, however, that what Moses allowed (tolerated) was contrary to that (v. 8). The disciples' reaction (vv. 10-12) shows that what Jesus taught (v. 9) was more rigid than what Moses tolerated. Thus they are not the same. Also in verse 12, Jesus's teaching included a reference to being an eunuch for the *kingdom's* sake. That doesn't sound like an explanation of the old law.

If Deuteronomy 24 meant that God approved of divorce for fornication, then what was allowed was not for the hardness of the Jews' heart. Obviously, Deuteronomy 22 and 24 are not the same as Matthew 5 and 19. Notice chart number 18.

According to the supporters of this position: (1) Jesus appeals to the beginning, (2) shows what Moses taught was contrary to that, and (3) then endorses what Moses said by explaining it in Matthew 19:9. Who can believe it?

Deut. 22 & 24	Matt. 5 & 19
1. Could not put away with approval.	1. Could put away with approval.
2. Not fornication for the fornicator was stoned (Deut. 22).	2. Cause was fornication.
3. Defiled if remarries.	3. Allow to remarry.

18

2. "The exception is not repeated by an apostle after Pentecost; thus it is not binding under the new covenant."

This is an arbitrary rule that says a thing must be repeated after Pentecost or it is not binding. What biblical basis is there for it? How would we know that the apostles had power to bind on earth were it not for Matthew's account? I wonder where the statements found in Matthew 18:17 and John 3:5 are repeated after Pentecost.

The apostles taught what they had heard from the Lord (Heb. 2:3). In 1 Corinthians 7:10 Paul did not repeat all that the Lord said, but he quotes part of his teaching and endorses it.

3. "In Matthew 5:32 and 19:9, Jesus was changing the law of Moses; yet what he taught was still of the old covenant."

If that be true, he did what he denied doing (Matt. 5:17). The old law said that fornicators and adulterers were to be stoned to death (Deut. 22). Thus, if he altered that, he did destroy the law.

**4. "Jesus pointed back to the beginning and endorsed it (Matt. 19:4-5). There was no exception then; thus none now. Jesus appealed to God's unchangeable moral law. No moral law ever changes."

It is true that Jesus pointed to the beginning and that he intends for marriage to be permanent. However, if God's law at the beginning wouldn't allow an exception, then we have Jesus (v. 9) at variance with the Father (Gen. 1-2). Did Jesus endorse something wrong?

Though Jesus does point to the beginning (vv. 4-5), he also uttered the words found in verse 9. He gives God's law from the beginning and then adds the only exception (which was no part of the law of Moses).

If an exception to a general rule is wholly contrary to moral law, then we have Jesus sanctioning that which is contrary to God's law at the beginning! Actually, the thing that was not true from the beginning (v. 8) was putting away for "every cause" (v. 3).

5. "Matthew 19:9 was spoken to the Jews. It applied to them and not to us."

The Pharisees didn't just ask about themselves, but man in general — "a man..." (v. 3). When Jesus answers, he speaks of "male and female" at the beginning and not merely of the Jews. In verse 9 "whosoever" includes far more than the Pharisees and the rest of the Jews. That same terminology is used in Romans 10:10-13 to describe those to whom salvation had been offered. Does it include only the Jews? Obviously not. Salvation was offered to Jews and Gentiles alike. Thus, the "whosoever" of Matthew 19:9 applies to Jews and Gentiles alike.

It is also true that the statements found in John 3:5; Matthew 22:35; 18:15-17 and John 4:24 were spoken to Jews. Does that mean they do not apply to us?

6. "There are differences in Matthew 19 and Mark 10. Matthew 19 was spoken to the Jews while Mark 10 was to the disciples. Mark 10:11-12 was spoken in the house while Matthew 19:9 was not. Matthew 19 contains the exception phrase and Mark 10 does not. Mark 10 applies today and Matthew 19 does not."

It is true that there are some differences in the accounts just as there are between Matthew 28 and Mark 16. However, that does not mean one is binding and the other is not.

Matthew's account deals with the question of putting away "for every cause," thus giving the only cause — fornication. Mark's account deals with the question of "putting away," thus no mention of a scriptural cause.

MacKnight suggests, "This 9th verse of Matthew seems to be parallel to the 11th verse of Mark, having been spoken to the disciples in the house, as is probable from the unusual change of persons observable in this part of the discourse" (*A Harmony of the Four Gospels* II:325-326). *Alford's Greek New Testament* (I:194) indicates the same idea.

This argument sounds a lot like the denominationalist who says that, since baptism is not mentioned in a certain passage, it must not be essential. These brethren say that, since the exception phrase is not found in Mark 10 and Luke 16, it is not binding.

This kind of contention puts Jesus and our friends in a predicament for we have Jesus approving for the Jews something we are told is fundamentally (and morally) untrue.

7. "The exception phrase is an interpolation; it was added by a scribe. It doesn't belong in Matthew 19:9."

There is no textural evidence to reject the phrase (cf. comments on this phrase in Lessons

3 and 4). Keep in mind that it is still supported by Matthew 5:32 as well as both the majority and minority type of Greek texts of Matthew 19:9. The 47 scholars of the KJV, 101 of the ASV, and 119 of the NKJV saw fit to include it as a part of the text.

8. "'Fornication' always refers to unlawful intercourse between unmarried people. Thus, Matthew 19:9 is not teaching that a man can put away his wife who is sexually unfaithful, for that is adultery. Matthew 19:9 refers to unlawful sexual relations before marriage, thus explaining Deuteronomy 22."

We defined "fornication" in Lesson 2 as "illicit sexual intercourse in general" (Thayer, 532). It is not limited to the unmarried. When the Corinthian church had a problem with a man having "his father's wife" it was called "fornication" (1 Cor. 5:1). In both the Old and New Testaments the term "fornication" is applied to the married as well as the unmarried (Num. 25:1-2; Amos 7:17; Ezek. 16:6, 23; Hos. 2:5; 1 Cor. 10:8; Rev. 2:14, 20). In fact, in Ezekiel 16:15, 29 God put his *wife* away for *fornication*. Even in the text under study (Matt. 19:9), the one who is put away for fornication is one who has been married (i.e., "put away his *wife*").

9. "Marriage is closer than a child-parent relationship; hence it can't be dissolved. (a) Close relationships can only be severed by death. (b) The husband-wife relationship is the closest of all. (c) Thus, that relationship is only severed by death. If something other than death can sever it, then it is not as close as the parent-child relationship."

This whole argument is based upon assumption. The very nature of the two relationships are different. One is a blood relation and the other is not. One is by choice or will and the other is not. For this argument to mean anything, it must first be proven that the nature of the two things compared are the same. That cannot be done. This is much like comparing water with mineral spirits. One may cut and clean some things while the other affects other things. However, that proves nothing about the comparative strengths and weaknesses of either one. Let us not forget that God put Israel away (severed that relationship) for fornication (Jer. 3; Ezek. 16).

10. "Romans 7:1-3 doesn't include the exception found in Matthew 5:32 and 19:9; thus the exception must not apply under the new covenant."

Romans 7 simply states the general or blanket rule. We must take all that the Bible says on this and any subject. Thus, Romans 7 isn't all that is stated on the subject. Matthew 19:9 reveals the exception to the general rule. An exception isn't a violation of the rule (cf. Lesson 4, section I). This argument is like contending that baptism is not essential because it is not mentioned in 1 John 5:1, John 3:16, or Luke 13:3.

Divorce and remarriage is not the subject of Romans 7. The theme is law and sin. The first three verses just illustrate how that one cannot be married to Christ unless he is dead to the old law. Otherwise, he is guilty of spiritual adultery. Mentioning the exception here would serve no purpose. "We must not fall into the mistake of loading his illustration with more significance than reasonably belongs to it in the context" (John Murray, *Divorce* 79).

11. "1 Corinthians 7:10-11 forbids remarriage and no exception is given. One is given only two choices: celibacy or reconciliation."

Again, this text gives us the blanket rule; the exception to it will be found in Matthew 5:32 and 19:9. If we can take this passage and conclude that it contains the sum of the New Testament doctrine on divorce and remarriage, then we can do the same with John 3:16 and 1 John 5:1 and the doctrine on conditions of salvation. If not, why not? Obviously, we must take all the Bible says on any subject to arrive at truth.

A few other quibbles are made in an effort to support this position, however, we have examined the major arguments that are presented.

NOTES

Questions

A verse to remember: "But I say unto you, That whosoever shall put away his wife, saving for the cause of fornication, causeth her to commit adultery: and whosoever shall marry her that is divorced committeth adultery" (Matt. 5:32).

Discussion

1. Discuss the possible motives behind the position being reviewed in this lesson. _____

2. Discuss the different forms of this position. _____

3. What significance does God's dealing with Israel bear on this lesson? _____

4. Discuss the idea that nothing is binding unless it is repeated after Pentecost and how it is refuted. _____

5. Discuss the difference between Deuteronomy 22 and 24 and Matthew 5 and 19. _____

True or False

_____ 1. The term "fornication" refers only to unlawful intercourse of unmarried people.

_____ 2. Divorce and remarriage is the subject of Romans 7:1-3.

_____ 3. The exception (putting away for fornication) does not apply after Pentecost.

_____ 4. Only Matthew and Mark include the exception phrase.

_____ 5. The exception found in Matthew 5:32 is not repeated after Pentecost.

_____ 6. Israel committed fornication (spiritually), but God never put her away.

Find the Passage

1. "... Hast thou seen that which backsliding Israel hath done? ... and there hath played the harlot ... backsliding Israel committed adultery I had put her away, and given her a bill of divorce...." _____

2. "And Jesus went about all Galilee, teaching in their synagogues, and preaching the gospel of the kingdom...." _____

3. "And unto the married I command, yet not I, but the Lord, Let not the wife depart from her husband: But and if she depart, let her remain unmarried, or be reconciled to her husband: and let not the husband put away his wife." _____

4. "For the woman which hath an husband is bound by the law to her husband so long as he liveth; but if the husband be dead, she is loosed from the law of her husband." _____

5. "Thou hast also committed fornication with the Egyptians thy neighbors...." _____

6. "But I say unto you, That whosoever shall put away his wife, saving for the cause of fornication, causeth her to commit adultery: and whosoever shall marry her that is divorced committeth adultery." _____

Answer in a Few Words

1. How do we know that Matthew 5:32 applies today? _____
2. How do we know that Matthew 19:9 applies today? _____
3. What does "fornication" mean? _____
4. Give a couple of reasons why Matthew 19:9 could not be an explanation of Deuteronomy 22 and 24.
   _____
5. Why is the exception not mentioned in Mark 10 and Romans 7? _____

Multiple Choice

_____ 1. The exception phrase is found only in (a) Matthew 19:9, (b) Deuteronomy 24:1-4, (c) Matthew 5:32 and 19:9, (d) Mark 10:11-12.

_____ 2. Matthew 19:9 (a) applies under the old covenant, (b) applies today, (c) applies today because every part of it is repeated after Pentecost.

_____ 3. Matthew 5:32 and 19:9 teach that (a) no divorce or remarriage is permissible, (b) divorce for fornication and then remarriage is permitted, (c) divorce for fornication is allowed, but no remarriage is permitted.

_____ 4. The exception phrase (a) is an interpolation, (b) is supported by both the minority and majority text, (c) is found only in the KJV.

_____ 5. Matthew 19:9 applies (a) only to the Jews, (b) only to the disciples, (c) to all men.

Fill in the Blank

1. Some teach that only _____ severs the bond.
2. God put _____ away for _____ (____ 16:26; Jer. ____:____).
3. The _____ rule is that divorce and remarriage is sin; one _____ to the rule is when the divorce is for _____.
4. _____ and _____ are the only passages that mention the exception.
5. Fornication is "Illicit sexual intercourse _____ _____."
6. Complete the chart --------->

_____	Matt. 5 & 19
1. _____ _____ put away with approval.	1. _____ put away with approval.
2. Not _____ for the fornicator was stoned (Deut. 22).	2. Cause was _____.
3. _____ if remarries.	3. _____ to remarry.

Lesson 7

Divorce for Any Cause without Remarriage, Divorce and Remarriage for Any Cause and Separation

Verses to remember: *"And unto the married I command, yet not I, but the Lord, Let not the wife depart from her husband: But and if she depart, let her remain unmarried, or be reconciled to her husband: and let not the husband put away his wife"* (1 Cor. 7:10-11).

The previous lesson dealt with an extreme view that prohibits divorce where God allows it. This lesson looks at the other end of the spectrum which allows divorce where God does not.

Some of our brethren offer what appears to be easy solutions to marital problems. One is, that when a couple fuss and fight and have lost their love for each other, they may get a divorce as long as they don't remarry. Another is that, if they are incompatible and no fornication has been committed, then, at least, they can separate. Our purpose is to examine these and related ideas to see if they are scriptural.

Divorce for Any Cause

Again, the idea is that, if the couple can't get along (incompatible) and they just don't love each other anymore, they can make a mutual decision to just call it quits and still be approved of God. This is argued by a number of brethren: that a divorce for any cause is scriptural as long as the parties don't remarry.

In searching for the answer, we are not left to human reasoning. God has not left man to decide for himself (Jer. 10:23). Thus, there are things that seem right to man, but are not pleasing to God (Prov. 16:25). The reason being that God's ways are higher than ours (Isa. 55:8-9). Go back and reconsider these points in Lesson 1.

God hates divorce (Mal. 2:13-16). Even divorce for fornication (which he approves, Matt. 19:9) is not a pleasant sight. Several passages forbid divorce for any other cause.

1. Matthew 19:3-12.

The question: The discussion about divorce and remarriage in this chapter began with a question that the Pharisees asked in verse 3, "Is it lawful for a man to put away his wife for every cause?" Notice that the question was about *divorce* for every cause, with nothing said about remarriage. Now if the answer to that question was yes, why didn't Jesus say yes? Rather, he dealt with the permanency of marriage in verses 4-6. These verses give four reasons one can't put away his mate for every cause. (1) God created one man for one woman. (2) Mates must cleave to each other. (3) A man and his wife are one flesh. (4) God has joined man and woman together in marriage. For a more detailed discussion of these four arguments, look back to Lesson 3. The answer that Jesus gave to the question was *no*.

A command not to divorce: Jesus said, "What therefore God hath joined together, let not man put asunder" (Matt. 19:6). In light of the question (v. 3), Jesus not only does not permit, but plainly prohibits divorce for just any cause, whether there is remarriage or not.

One exception: In verse 9 our Lord gives one exception to the rule stated above, that being fornication. "It is not the exceptive clause that bears the weight of the emphasis in the text. It is rather that the husband may not put away *for any other cause*" (John Murray, *Divorce* 21). When a man puts away his wife for some cause other than fornication, while he is not guilty of adultery until he remarries, he is guilty of the sin of putting her away for an unscriptural cause.

2. Matthew 5:32.

One cause: This passage, like Matthew 19:9, states only one cause for divorce — fornication. Remarriage on the part of the one who puts away is not even discussed in this passage. Still, only one cause is given.

Causes her to commit adultery: When a man puts away his wife for any cause other than fornication, he "causeth her to commit adultery." He sins against her by unjustly putting her in a position where she will commit adultery if she remarries. "Our Lord is no doubt regarding the woman from the station or position in which she is placed by the divorce. She is placed in the position either of being tempted to be joined to another man or being plied with solicitations to union on the part of another man, or indeed, of both. Our Lord is fully cognizant of the weakness of human nature and of the great liability to another marital undertaking on the part of the divorced woman" (Murray 24).

It may be thought that since the man who puts away his wife (for a cause other than fornication) doesn't remarry and thus is not guilty of adultery, that he has not sinned. It is true that "the divorcing husband is not charged with being an adulterer" (Murray, 24), however, he is charged with wrongdoing. When adultery results, he is the cause and bears the guilt.

3. 1 Corinthians 7:10-11.

Terms defined: These verses are discussing divorce and not separation. The word translated "depart" is the same word translated "put asunder" in Matthew 19:6. Thayer says it means "to separate, divide, part, put asunder: ... Matt. xix.6 ... of divorce ... 1 Co. vii.11" (674). Bauer says "be separated of divorce ... 1 Cor. 7:10" (890). This point is clearly seen in that when she does *depart* she is *unmarried* (v. 11).

Contrast in who spoke: In verses 10-11 Paul said, "I command, yet not I, but the Lord." But, in verses 12ff. he says, "But to the rest speak I, not the Lord." Though there is a contrast in who spoke what, one section is just as authoritative as the other. "In verses 10, 11 Paul says (in effect), 'I am repeating — in a concrete way — the principle about divorce that the Lord (Jesus Christ) set forth in his teaching when He was with the disciples and spoke about divorce among God's people: But in verses 12-16, he says (in effect), 'Now I am going to deal with a question that did not arise, and, therefore, that Jesus did not mention when He lived among us. This issue has arisen now that the gospel has gone out among pagans, and I shall address myself to it on my own (in an inspired way, of course, just as I have spoken of many other questions of this sort in this very letter)'" (Jay E. Adams, *Marriage, Divorce and Remarriage,* 37).

Emphatic prohibition: This text not only does not allow divorce for any cause, but also contains several statements that forbid it. Verse 10 says, "Let not the wife depart from her husband." Verse 11 states, "Let not the husband put away his wife." Verse 12, "let him not put her away." Verse 13, "let her not leave him." Simply put, he says, "Don't do it!"

Keep in mind also that 1 Corinthians 7:10-11 say nothing about remarriage on the part of the one who puts away. Thus, the prohibition is not only applied in the event he plans to remarry. The divorce is forbidden (remarriage or not).

4. The Bible is silent concerning other causes.

Fornication is the only cause for divorce that is authorized (Matt. 19:9). There is no mention of any other cause. Thus, one cannot divorce for just any cause for the same reason that the Lord could not be a priest on earth: "of which" the Lord "spake nothing" (Heb. 7:14). To act without authority in this realm is just as wrong as using instrumental music in worship.

5. Any passage on the husband-wife relationship (e.g. love) forbids divorce for any cause.

Divorce is contrary to the divine institution, contrary to the nature of marriage, and contrary to the divine action by which the union is effected. It is precisely here that its wickedness becomes singularly apparent — it is the sundering by man of a union God has constituted (John Murray, *Divorce*, 33).

Principles of the husband loving his wife (Eph. 5:25) and the wife loving her husband (Tit. 2:4) are violated when divorce is obtained for just any cause. Paul argues in Romans 7:1-4 that "the woman which hath an husband is bound by the law to her husband so long as he liveth." Thus, it is not a relationship that can be severed at will.

6. Arguments made to justify divorce for any cause as long as one does not remarry.

a. "Matthew 5:32; 19:9; Mark 10:11-12 and Luke 16:18 discuss divorce and remarriage. That is what is condemned."

We have already noticed that in Matthew 19 the question was not about remarriage, but divorce. Jesus answered that question saying *no* (vv. 4-6). It is not until verse 9 that he introduces remarriage. Even then, the only cause for divorce in the whole chapter (or Bible for that matter) is fornication.

I also remind you that Matthew 5:32 does not discuss remarriage on the part of the one who puts away. Thus, the above argument is just not so. Even if the argument stands, there is still no authority in these passages or any other for divorce for just any cause. (For more on the logical conclusions of this argument, see the appendix.)

b. "In 1 Corinthians 7:10-11 the phrase 'but and if she depart' indicates that divorce is approved as long as they either remain unmarried or are reconciled."

If such is true, it plainly contradicts the prohibitions in the context. "Paul is not allowing exceptions from the rule of Christ, but advising in cases where the mischief was done" (*Expositor's Greek Testament*, II: 825). The phrase under question does not grant permission, but simply introduces what is to be done if one does violate the prohibition.

Consider 1 John 2:1 as a parallel passage as far as construction is concerned. Here the subject is *sin*. First, there is the prohibition "these things write I unto you, that ye sin not." Then, the next statement is "And if any man sin, we have an advocate with the Father, Jesus Christ the righteous." When John says, "If any man sin," he does not give liberty to sin nor mean that God will approve of it when you do. He is simply discussing how we can be forgiven in the event that we do sin. Likewise, 1 Corinthians 7:10-11 does not suggest any liberty to divorce, but only states what is to be done when such occurs.

This argument with which we are dealing "is plainly an example of an appeal to one part of a text in neglect of the clear import of the other part, and, in this instance, of appeal to the part that is distinctly subordinate and contingent in neglect of the part that is unconditional and primary" (John Murray, *Divorce*, 56).

> He is saying in effect, "If separation (divorce, DVR) has actually taken place, then certain provisions must be adhered to. Let the breach be healed. Failing that, under no condition may another marriage be undertaken: In other words, the parenthesis simply regulates the wrong when it has taken place but does not in the least legitimate the separation (divorce, DVR) itself" (Murray, 62).

There is some question as to whether "but and if she depart" is active or passive and whether past or future. For a discussion of that see the appendix in the back of the book. "Whether she initiates the divorce action or he, is not the point here; rather, the aorist passive conveys the general pronouncement (as found in the teaching of Jesus on the matter, cf. Matt. 19:3-12) that the woman is not to be divorced from her husband" (Maurice W. Lusk, III, *The Southeastern Evangelist* 9:3, March 1980).

It is further argued that though no permission is given to divorce, that if one does he is in an approved state as long as he either remains unmarried or is reconciled. That is mere assumption! He is not in any approved condition until he repents of the *SIN* of putting away his mate for an unscriptural cause. This contention assumes the very point to be proven: that divorce for some cause other than fornication is scriptural.

No Permission Or Approval Given

1 John 2:1	1 Cor. 7:10-11
"...sin not..."	"...depart not..."
(The Prohibition)	(The Prohibition)
"...if any man sin..."	"...if she depart..."
(No Permission)	(No Permission)

It is also assumed that "unmarried" and "reconciled" are equally desirable states or conditions. The text doesn't indicate that they are. Reconciliation requires the cooperation of both spouses, thus an alternative is given (remain unmarried) in the event that reconciliation is unavailable. "She must remain unmarried (i.e. not marry another) so that she will be in a position at all times to repent and be reconciled to her husband" (Jay E. Adams, *Marriage, Divorce And Remarriage*, 41).

Divorce and Remarriage for Any Cause

This position is basically the same as the previous one, except this one does not forbid remarriage. If the couple can't get along or the love is gone, then it is scriptural to get a divorce (again, no fornication involved). And, if there is remarriage no sin has been committed, we are told. I am not aware of any brother that advocates this position; however, I'm sure there are some who would agree with it.

Jesus plainly denies this. In his teaching, the Lord only gives one cause (fornication) for divorce (Matt. 5:32; 19:9). It is clearly stated that if a man puts away his wife (for any cause other than fornication) and marries another he is guilty of adultery (Matt. 19:9; Mark. 10:11-12; Luke 16:18).

To remain unmarried. We have already noticed from 1 Corinthians 7:10-11 that if he does divorce and reconciliation is unavailable, he is not permitted to marry again, but is to remain unmarried.

Some have argued from 1 Corinthians 7:27-28 (which says, "... Art thou loosed from a wife? Seek not a wife. But and if thou marry, thou hast not sinned...") that, if one is divorced (loosed), he does not sin in remarrying. However, with a little consideration, it is obvious that verse 28 does not include anyone who may decide to marry or remarry, but only those who have been given the right. Otherwise, this text would contradict such passages as Matthew 19:9 and Romans 7:1-3. If this verse (v. 28) gives *anyone* who divorces or is divorced the right to remarry, then no one who remarried would be guilty of adultery. And besides, in the first part of verse 27 when Paul says "seek not to be loosed," he means "'Do not be seeking release' (*lusin*) from the marriage bond..." (A.T. Robertson, *Word Pictures in the New Testament,* IV: 132). But, when he says, "Art thou loosed from a wife? Seek not a wife," the word "loosed" is from a different word. "Bachelors as well as widowers are included in *lelusai....* This advice of Paul he only urges 'because of the present necessity' (verse 26)" (A.T. Robertson, *Ibid.,* 132; cf. *The Expositor's Greek Testament,* II: 832). Thus, in the first part of verse 27, "loosed" refers to divorce, whereas in the second part "loosed" refers not to divorce, but to one who has never been married or his mate is dead.

Divorce and Remarriage for Any Legal Cause

The idea here is that if the cause for divorce is legal (in harmony with civil law), it is scriptural. There is really no difference in this and the previous section in view of "no fault" divorce. Keep in mind that, even if in your state there is "no fault divorce," in reality there is some real reason for the divorce, e.g. fornication, incompatibility, physical, or mental cruelty.

This position would make the law of man more binding than the law of God, which forbids divorce for just any cause. Without repeating all that has already been said, let us be reminded that the New Testament gives only *one cause* despite what civil courts or laws may say.

Though one may divorce and remarry and be *legal,* Romans 7:1-3 shows that if it is not according to the Scriptures, he is still *bound* to his first mate and thus guilty of adultery.

What about Separation?

The idea among some is that when marital problems arise, it is true that the couple can't get a divorce (when there is no fornication), but they can just separate.

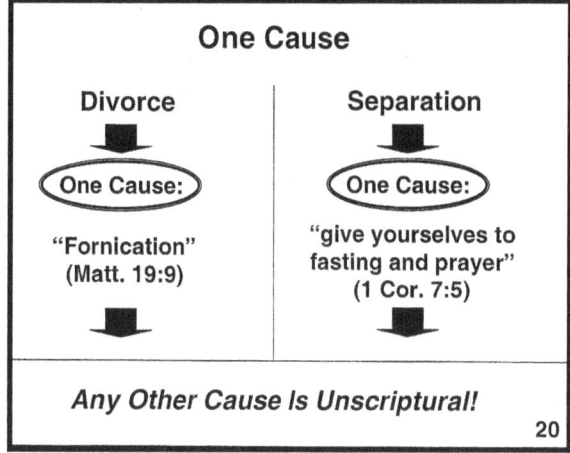

1. Separation defined. Separation is not the same as divorce, though we sometimes use the terms interchangeably. It simply refers to a couple not living together as husband and wife, though they are still married. This may take place in various forms of deliberate refusal to live as a normal couple. It would include complete desertion, one of them running home to "mama," living in separate bedrooms under the same roof and even deliberately abstaining from intercourse.

2. Only one passage addresses the subject. This writer only knows of one passage that discusses separation, that being 1 Corinthians 7:5. It says, "Defraud ye not one the other, except it be with consent for a time, that ye may give yourselves to fasting and prayer; and come together again, that Satan tempt you not for your incontinency."

While some question whether that verse really addresses separation, I believe that in some way it touches upon the subject. Some think that 1 Corinthians 7:10-11 involves separation, however we have already shown that it doesn't.

3. Only one cause given. The separation in our text is to "give yourselves to fasting and prayer." There is no other cause given in this text or any other. To separate for any other reason is unscriptural, just as is divorce for any cause other than fornication.

There are some *conditions* laid down besides the cause. (1) It is to be "with consent." There must be the approval of both spouses. (2) Part of the agreement is "for a time," i.e., the separation is to only be for an agreed short time. Thus the couple is not to separate indefinitely with no idea how long it will last. (3) This is to be done in view of and in agreement to "come together again."

If one contends that one can separate for any other cause than the one mentioned in 1 Corinthians 7:5 (and under any other conditions), the burden of proof is upon him to find where the Bible so teaches.

4. "What if the love is gone or the couple just can't get along or the husband drinks?" This is something that must be considered before marriage. The two had better make sure marriage is what they really want, and if it is, decide they are going to make it work.

There are no provisions in the New Testament for separation for these causes. The concept with which we are dealing is contrary to all of the passages on love and cleaving in marriage.

5. Separation usually causes more problems than it solves. Listen to Jay E. Adams, long time marital counselor:

Modern separation settles nothing, it amounts to a refusal to face issues and set them at rest. The world may have no way of solving problems — and so opts for an easy cease fire — but the church does, if she will only avail herself of the biblical means. ... It keeps all parties involved on the end of the line, playing them like a fish in the water dancing on its tail. It violates the command in 1 Cor. 7:5, disregards its warning and sets both husband and wife in a place of unnecessary temptation. ... Can separation provide for a "cooling off period" as some claim? Hardly ... moreover, every counselor knows that the way to put people together is not by taking them apart. Separation heats up desire that it shouldn't, but cools concern that it ought not. ... Two people, under separate roofs, will find it nearly impossible to solve problems that occur when they are under the same roof. Separation, therefore, only widens gaps and deepens difficulties (*Marriage, Divorce and Remarriage* 33-34).

6. "What about a case where the wife is beaten by her husband or suffers some other physical cruelty?" We are not to let an emotional plea or "situation ethics" determine our answer. If that kind of plea justifies one thing it would justify anything. It is possible to allow human reasoning to make God's requirements on this or any other matter seem unreasonable.

If I *assume* that the woman can leave her husband for this reason, or any other, besides the one of 1 Corinthians 7:5, then I must also assume the conditions under which it can be done. The question is, where do I draw the line — with something I find in the book of God or upon human reasoning? If upon the Bible, let's discuss it in light of a verse of Scripture. If upon human reasoning, what's to keep us from "reasoning" that separation for any cause and under any condition is all right?

As we deal with this question, we must remember that there is but one cause for separation given in the New Testament (1 Cor. 7:5). Concerning others, the Bible is silent.

Admittedly, this is not an easy question to answer. I may have my own ideas about what I

NOTES

would do if I were a woman in that situation or if my own daughter were to be the one involved. I would probably leave and want my daughter to also. I can't help but be sympathetic with the abused spouse. However, *I can't preach by faith that God approves* of the separation, because I can't find it in the New Testament.

Don't misunderstand. This does not mean that she can't protect herself (and her children) by calling the law when she is abused by her husband just as she could if any other mad man abused her.

On the other hand, it is easy to see how that an abusive mate who runs his mate off and drives her out of the house is responsible for the separation and not the one who was forced to leave.

7. Arguments made to justify separation. (1) "The responsibility to one's mate is parallel to obeying parents; there are some circumstances that justify doing otherwise." Obeying one's parents is not an unqualified requirement. Rather, it is "in the Lord" (Eph. 6:1). Every command from man (whether from parents, civil authorities or one's employer) is qualified by Acts 5:29 (obey God rather than man). Separation, on the other hand, does not violate a command from man, but one from God (1 Cor. 7:5). (2) "If one can't live with his spouse and still be a Christian, then separation is permissible." This begs the very question to be proven. It assumes one can't be a Christian and remain. This contention also assumes that one can violate one command (1 Cor. 7:5) to fulfill another duty of Christian service (cf. Rom. 3:8).

May God help us to learn the seriousness of marriage and that it cannot be destroyed at our will and God be pleased.

Questions

A verse to remember: "Defraud ye not one the other, except it be with consent for a time, that ye may give yourselves to fasting and prayer; and come together again, that Satan tempt you not for your incontinency" (1 Cor. 7:5).

Discussion

1. Discuss the difference in divorce and separation. _____
   _____

2. What are some consequences of the position that says divorce is permissible as long as there is no remarriage? _____
   _____

3. Discuss the contrast in "I command, yet not I, but the Lord" (1 Cor. 7:10) and "But to the rest speak I, not the Lord" (1 Cor. 7:12). _____
   _____

4. Why do you think we have lost sight of the rule and emphasized the exception in Matthew 19:9?
   _____
   _____

5. In what sense is the put away woman made an adulteress (Matt. 5:32)? _____
   _____

6. How do passages on love and the husband/wife relationship forbid divorce for any cause? _____
   _____

True or False

_____ 1. Matthew 5:32 does mention remarriage on the part of the one who puts away.

_____ 2. 1 Corinthians 7:10-11 does not discuss divorce.

_____ 3. The expression "but and if she depart" (1 Cor. 7:11) grants permission to divorce.

_____ 4. "Unmarried" and "be reconciled" (1 Cor. 7:11) are equally desirable states or conditions.

_____ 5. 1 Corinthians 7:5 is the only passage that discusses separation.

Find the Passage

1. "Art thou bound unto a wife? Seek not to be loosed. Are thou loosed from a wife? Seek not a wife. But and if thou marry, thou hast not sinned...." _____

2. "For the Lord, the God of Israel, saith that he hateth putting away...." _____

3. "Defraud ye not one the other, except it be with consent for a time, that ye may give yourselves to fasting and prayer; and come together again, that Satan tempt you not for your incontinency." ___

4. "What therefore God hath joined together, let not man put asunder." _____

5. "And unto the married I command, yet not I, but the Lord, Let not the wife depart from her husband: But and if she depart, let her remain unmarried, or be reconciled to her husband: and let not the husband put away his wife." _____

6. "For it is evident that our Lord sprang out of Juda; of which tribe Moses spake nothing concerning priesthood." _____

Answer in a Few Words

1. What is the cause for separation given in 1 Corinthians 7:5? _____
2. List the conditions under which separation may take place as they are given in 1 Corinthians 7:5.
   _____
3. How do you know that 1 Corinthians 7:10-11 discusses divorce and not separation? _____
   _____
4. List the passages that forbid divorce for any cause. _____
5. Define separation. _____

Multiple Choice

_____ 1. God allows separation (a) for incompatibility, (b) for any reason, (c) for a season to give time to fasting and prayer.

_____ 2. If a couple separates under the conditions of 1 Corinthians 7:5, it (a) doesn't matter how long they are separated, (b) must only be for an agreed time, (c) poses no danger for them.

_____ 3. When Jesus responded to the Pharisees' question (Matt. 19:3-12), his answer was (a) that divorce is not permitted for every cause, (b) that divorce for any cause is all right, (c) that divorce for just any cause is all right only if there is no remarriage.

_____ 4. The man who puts away his wife for some cause other than fornication is (a) guilty of adultery, (b) approved of God, (c) guilty of sin, though not the sin of adultery.

_____ 5. When a couple can no longer get along, they may (a) divorce and remarry, (b) divorce, so long as neither remarry, (c) separate, but not divorce, (d) neither divorce nor separate.

Fill in the Blank

1. Though we can be sympathetic with some who feel that they must separate for some cause other than the one of 1 Corinthians 7:5, we can't _____ it by _____ because we can't find it in the ____ _____.

2. Murray correctly said that is not the _____ clause of Matthew 19:9 that bears the weight of emphasis, but the fact that the husband may not put away _____ _____ _____ _____.

3. The separation of 1 Corinthians 7:5 is so that each spouse may give his/herself to _____ and _____.

4. When a couple scripturally separates, it is to be _____ _____ and for a _____ and that they may _____ _____ again.

5. Divorce for any cause is forbidden when Paul said, "Let _____ the wife _____ from her husband ... and let _____ the _____ _____ _____ his wife."

Lesson 8

Mental Divorce
(May Some Put Away People Remarry?)

Verses to remember: *"For Herod himself had sent forth and laid hold upon John, and bound him in prison for Herodias' sake, his brother Philip's wife: for he had married her. For John had said unto Herod, It is not lawful for thee to have thy brother's wife"* (Mark 6:17-18).

In recent years there have been differences among brethren concerning whether some put away people could remarry. In previous chapters, we have stated that no put away person can remarry. There are several among us who believe otherwise. They would not affirm that all put away ones could remarry, but only certain ones.

Actually this is an effort by some to justify remarriage following an unlawful divorce. The details of this position will be given later.

I realize that the position I take has its consequences and raises some questions. However, I am willing to face those. I also realize that this chapter is a little longer than the others. I feel that this particular aspect of the divorce and remarriage question is worthy of the extra space.

The Position Stated

This position states that some put away people can remarry (e.g. one put away for some cause other than fornication whose mate remarries first). In application it says that when Jack puts away Jill (for being a poor cook) that, though that is a civil divorce, they are not really divorced. It is called a divorce only "accommodatively." If Jack then remarries another woman, he, being guilty of adultery, can be put away *mentally* by Jill. This is the "real" divorce. Now she is free to remarry. Some would suggest that, in this case, Jill would have to have fought the divorce all the way.

Some of our brethren have signed their names to affirm the following propositions:

The Scriptures teach that when a man puts away his wife for any cause other than fornication and he subsequently marries another that his first wife then may put him away for fornication and she has the scriptural right to remarry another.

The Scriptures teach that the innocent person (free of fornication) who has been put away without God's or his/her approval and against whom adultery has been committed may remarry.

Confusion on "Marriage," "Bond," and "Divorce"

This position equates *marriage* and the *bond*. It says that, if one is married, he is bound; if one is divorced, he is loosed. Therefore a distinction is made between marriage (the same would apply for divorce) that is civil (in the eyes of man) and that is real (in the eyes of God). If it is scriptural, we are told that it is real. If it is unscriptural, it is called "marriage" or "divorce" only "accommodatively." This distinction is essential to the position. Carefully reread chapter five.

The case of Herod and Herodias demonstrates that marriage is marriage (real), whether God approves or not. The text says they were *married*, even though John said it was unlawful (Mark 6:17-18).

In Matthew 19:9 Jesus said that a man who divorces his wife, "puts her away," even though it is unscriptural. When he takes another wife, he calls it marriage even though it is unscriptural. From the one statement, "Whosoever shall *put away* his wife, except it be for fornication, and shall *marry another* committeth adultery" (emphasis mine, DVR), we learn two things. (1) A man who *puts away* his wife (for a cause other than fornication) and *marries* another commits adultery. (2) A man who *puts away* his wife (for fornication) and *marries* another does not commit adultery. The question I would like to ask the mental divorce advocates is what did Jesus mean when he used the expressions "put away" and "marry another"? Did he mean really put away or only accommodatively? Did he mean really marry another or only accommodatively? Remember that in the above statement that he only uses those expressions one time. Thus, if he means *really* divorced and remarried it has that meaning in points 1 *and* 2 above. If he meant they were divorced and remarried only *accommodatively* then it has that meaning in points 1 *and* 2 above. Our brethren are going to have to make up their minds. If we try to make it go both directions we make Jesus guilty of equivocating. Consider chart 17.

Is It Real or Not?

"And I say unto you, Whosoever shall put away his wife, except it be for fornication, and shall marry another, committeth adultery: and whoso marrieth her which is put away doth commit adultery."

Man — "Puts Away" Wife — Marries Another" — Adultery
(for cause other than fornication

Real? or Not?

Man — "Puts Away" Wife — "Marries Another" — No Adultery
(for fornication)

17

Jesus didn't inform his hearers that he was shifting back and forth from a real to an accommodative and back to a real use of those terms. If the mental divorce position be correct, it looks like Jesus could have told us just how he used the terms.

If an unscriptural divorce is not a real divorce in the eyes of God, then why did Jesus say "Whosoever shall put away his wife, *except...*"? The exception shows that it is possible to be divorced though it is not approved of God.

If those who contend for a distinction between marriage or divorce that is real (in the eyes of God) and that which is accommodative (only in the eyes of man) are correct, then Matthew 19:9 should read:

And I say unto you, Whosoever shall put away (divorce, actually) for the cause of fornication may marry (actually) another. Whosoever shall divorce (accommodatively speaking), without fornication as the cause, and shall marry (accommodatively speaking) committeth adultery (because he is not actually divorced and is actually married): Whoso marrieth her (accommodatively speaking) which is put away (accommodatively speaking) doth commit adultery (because she is not actually divorced). Yet if she which is divorced (accommodatively speaking) did not consent to the divorce (accommodatively speaking) she may mentally divorce (actually) so that he who marries her (actually) does not commit adultery (Gene Frost, *Gospel Anchor* [May 1982], 269).

Why not just take Jesus at his word when he says that she is put away and marries another (whether it is scriptural or not)? Something is wrong when we have to read "actual" or "accommodative" into the passage. Such confusion violates basic rules of interpretation.

There is no reason to say that "put away" or "marry" is used in an accommodative sense. A general rule of interpretation is that all words and sentences are to be taken literally unless for sound reasons they cannot be (cf. Robert Milligan, *Reason and Revelation,* 332).

How is figurative language determined?

1. The sense of the context will indicate it ... 2. A word or sentence is figurative when the literal meaning involves an impossibility ... 3. The language of Scripture may be regarded as figurative, if the literal interpretation will cause one passage to contradict another ... 4. When the scriptures are made to demand actions that are wrong, or forbid those that are good, they are supposed to be figurative ... 5. When it is said to be figurative ... 6. When the definite is put for the indefinite ... 7. When said in mockery ... 8. Common sense — Figures of speech sometimes occur when we have to depend on things we know, in order to decide if the language is figurative or literal (D.R. Dungan, *Hermeneutics* 195-202).

Romans 7:2-3 clearly shows a distinction between the *marriage* and the *bond*. Here a woman is bound to one while married to another. That is why the second marriage is adulterous. Note verse 3, "So then if, while her husband liveth, she be *married* to another man, she shall be called an adulteress: but if her husband be dead, she is free from that law; so that she is no adulteress, though she be married to another man" (emphasis mine, DVR). The first part of the verse describes an unscriptural situation, but says she is "married." The second part describes a scriptural situation and also says she is "married."

The point is just as clear from 1 Corinthians 7:10-11. When the divorce is unscriptural, the result is they are "unmarried." The mental divorce advocates would say, "No, no, they are still married in the eyes of God." However, Paul didn't say "remain married," but "remain unmarried."

We have given abundant proof that the "marriage" and the "bond" are not to be equated. *Marriage* and *divorce* refer to the physical relationship. In our time, both involve a legal process. *Bound* and *loose* refer to spiritual obligations before God.

I would like for those who are so minded as to equate the two to give us a definition of "divorce" and "marriage" that would apply to both those that have and those that don't have God's approval.

No Authority

The silence of the Scriptures must be respected. We must do all things by the authority of Jesus Christ (Col. 3:17). We must always act within the doctrine of Christ (2 John 9). To go onward and beyond what is authorized is to have not God. God's silence is not permission to act. Jesus could not be a priest on earth for he was of the tribe of Judah "of which tribe Moses spake nothing concerning priesthood" (Heb. 7:14). Thus, to do what is unauthorized is to sin. That's why it is wrong to have instrumental music in worship or put ice cream on the Lord's table.

There is no passage that authorizes any put away person to remarry. That person cannot remarry for the same reason that we do not use instrumental music in worship: *no authority!*

Furthermore, for the mental divorce concept to work there has to be a second putting away. Jack put Jill away for burning the bread. That is one putting away. He then remarries, thus giving her the right to mentally put him away (the second putting away) and remarry. The Bible is as silent about a second putting away as it is about the remarriage of a put away one.

The "Put Away" One Forbidden to Remarry

Not only does the Bible not authorize any put away one to remarry, but it emphatically forbids it.

The passages. "... and whosoever shall marry

her that is divorced committeth adultery" (Matt. 5:32b). "... and whoso marrieth her which is put away doth commit adultery" (Matt. 19:9b). "... and whosoever marrieth her that is put away from her husband committeth adultery" (Luke 16:18b).

From these statements I not only learn that the one who puts away his mate (for some cause other than fornication) and remarries commits adultery, but also the one who is *put away* commits adultery when he/she remarries. Chart 5 illustrates the above passages.

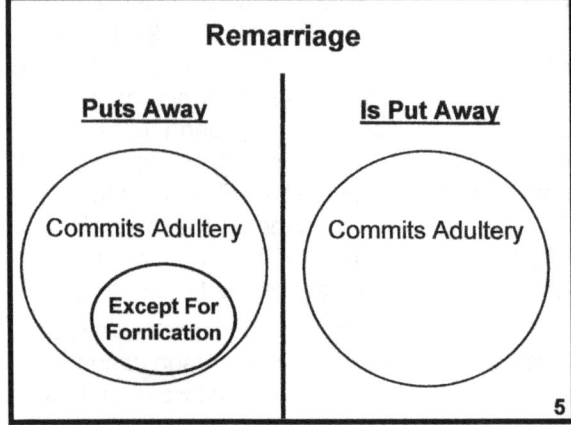

No exceptions. The exception phrase found in Matthew 5:32 and 19:9 applies to the one who puts away. There is no exception phrase with reference to the one who is put away. The text doesn't say, "Whosoever marrieth her that is put away (except 'her' that is put away against her wishes and whose mate remarries first) commits adultery."

The text says "and" not "or." In the clause, "and whoso marrieth her which is put away..." the *and* is a connective showing that both the one who puts away (without fornication) and the one put away commit adultery in a subsequent marriage. It is not the word "or," nor does it have that meaning. If it did, that would mean that whichever one married first commits adultery and not the other.

In 1986, I wrote to several scholars asking them if it were ever possible for this word "and" (Greek: *kai*) to be translated "or." Bruce Metzger said, "no." Zane Hodges said, "less likely." F. Wilbur Gingrich replied, "not likely." Sakae Kubo said, "'Or' could not be a translation of *kai* in that context."

Thus, the text says that the put away one commits adultery no matter who marries first. She may have fought the divorce and protested it till the end. However, the text says if she remarries she commits adultery.

Consider Luke 16:18, where the man who puts away his wife and marries another commits adultery. Why didn't Jesus say that she may now put him away mentally and remarry? Rather, he said, "and whosoever marrieth her that is put away from her husband committeth adultery."

It is argued that the word translated "and" (Greek: *kai*) means "likewise," i.e., the woman put away without fornication — her situation is like the man who put away his wife (without a scriptural cause). When either or both remarry, they commit adultery. This is an effort to say that this "put away" one (in the text) doesn't include all put away people. Thus, the argument concludes that the woman put away (unscripturally), whose husband then remarries, is not found in Matthew 5:32, 19:9, or Luke 16:18. When I hear or read this argument, I always wonder what the difference is in "likewise," "and," or "or." Granting that it means "likewise," what real difference is there in that and if we say it means "and"? I have no real problem with it meaning "likewise." Thayer says that the word *kai* can be so translated. If that is the case, chart 21 illustrates what Matthew 19:9 would say.

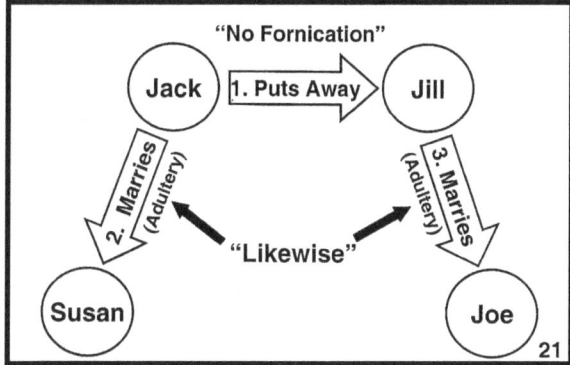

Notice that when Jill remarries she commits adultery just like Jack does. Look again at the text and see that Jack is one who not only unscripturally put Jill away, but also remarried. I fail to see how "likewise" really helps the mental divorce advocates, unless they really mean "or" when they use "likewise." In fact, it has to mean *or* to really fit their position.

It is also argued that the "and" (Greek: *kai*) is not "sequential," i.e., it doesn't suggest a sequence of events like: (1) Man puts away wife, (2) he remarries, (3) she remarries. It is an assumption that the events of the text are not sequential. However, it is not necessarily a sequence of events. The put away one who remarries commits adultery whether it is before or after his first mate remarries. So supposing that the clause, "and whoso marrieth her that is put away doth commit adultery," is isolated doesn't help the position one bit. It doesn't have to be sequential to fit the position we are presenting in this book.

Includes all put away ones. Since there is no exception phrase in Matthew 5:32b; 19:9b, and Luke 16:18b, *all* put away ones must be included. The put away fornicator cannot remarry. The one put away for a cause other than fornication cannot remarry. Therefore, all who have been put away are forbidden to remarry.

Again, it is argued that the "her" that is put away in these texts is not just any "her" that is put away. Rather, it is "her" that is put away without fornication being the cause. Thus, the one unscripturally put away whose husband has remarried is not included in the text. Granting that the first part of the verse limits the "her," remember we have already shown that would mean that the "her" is one whose husband has not only unscripturally put her away, but also remarried. And yet that is the very one that the mental divorce advocates say can remarry. Jesus said that she commits adultery if she does. The brother who makes this argument is the one who demands that the text must be "sequential" for he says that the "her" of Matthew 19:9b is the wife of "whosoever," of Matthew 19:9a. We must decide whether it is sequential or not.

Granting the whole argument to our brethren does not establish one ounce of authority for any put away one to remarry.

Is it just a race to the lawyer's office? If the put away one can't remarry, then it all boils down to who gets to the lawyer's office first. Right? Not necessarily! If the guilty party files for divorce the innocent can counter sue. One problem concerning the charge of a race to the lawyer's office is due to the fact that we are mistaking the "filing" for divorce (the intent) with the final "putting away."

Reverses the Order of the Text

According to Matthew 5:32 and 19:9 the one who has a right to remarry is one who has first put away his mate for fornication. Thus, the order is (1) fornication (on part of the mate), (2) put away the fornicator, and (3) remarry. The mental divorce position would have the divorce, then the fornication due to an unscriptural marriage and thus the innocent is free to remarry. That order would be (1) put away, (2) fornication, and (3) remarriage. The text doesn't say that after the putting away and adultery results, then the other mate is free to remarry. To pervert the order of this text is just as dangerous as to pervert Mark 16:16. Consider chart 10.

God's Order -vs- Man's Order

Mark 16:16

1. Believe   2. Bapticed   3. Saved

MAN:

1. Believe   2. Saved   3. Baptized

Matt. 19:9

1. Fornication   2. Put Away   3. Remarriage

MAN:

1. Put Away   2. Remarriage   3. Fornication
1. Put Away   2. Fornication   3. Remarriage

10

In response to the above, it is sometimes argued that Mark 10:9-11 gives another order (1) put away, (2) adultery, and (3) remarriage. However, there is *not one word in that text about remarriage on the part of the put away one!*

Consequences of This Position

If one is going to take the position that some put away people can remarry, he must be willing to accept the consequences.

Waiting game: If a woman is put away and "cannot contain" and thus remarries *before* he does, she is guilty of adultery. However, if she does not marry until *after* he marries first, she is not guilty of adultery we are told. This is the waiting game. She may have to wait him out ten years. But as soon as he remarries, she has the right to mentally put him away and remarry.

I wonder why some of these brethren don't think the man who puts away his wife (for a cause other than fornication) is free to remarry, if she remarried first.

Of course, the mental divorce advocates deny that they promote the waiting game. Some of them tell us that the put away one who has a right to remarry must have fought the divorce all the way. This, we are told, would discourage the waiting game. This assumes then that the woman of Matthew 19:9b wanted the divorce, which wouldn't fit the circumstances of that time. The Jewish woman, if divorced, couldn't get a job and had no way to support herself. So most Jewish women wouldn't want the divorce. Only Mark (written to Gentiles) mentions a woman getting a divorce. The Gentile economic situation would make it more likely that a Gentile woman would want a divorce.

This rule, that she must have opposed the divorce, is just an arbitrary rule made by the advocates of the position.

Mental marriages: If we can have "mental divorce" at one end, why not have "mental marriages" at the other, before the fact of legal and social requirements? A couple could cohabit as long as they are committed to each other and plan to meet the legal requirements. A young man and woman in an emotional and passionate state could decide they are married and thus be allowed to engage in intercourse with God's approval without social and legal requirements.

If the marriage and divorce can be mental, why couldn't the adultery also be mental especially in light of Matthew 5:28? If a man lusts after a woman, could he be scripturally put away?

Divorced and don't know it: It would be possible to be "really" divorced and not know it. If you are the one that put away your mate unscripturally and then remarried, you could be mentally put away by your first mate. Before that mental act you are "really" married. After that you are "really" divorced. Since it is a mental thing, your mate could put you away and you not even know it. You could still be married and not know it. Such reasoning throws the marriage state into utter chaos: married, divorced, and remarried at thought.

A second putting away: According to the position under review the put away one now puts away his mate. That is more than one putting away. Jesus didn't know anything about a second putting away. If a man puts away his innocent wife and then remarries, what more can she do in "putting him away" that he has not already done? If he has already terminated the marriage and the covenant what more can she do? She can't put him away if they are no longer married.

Both partners can remarry without sin: Those who also believe that the guilty party can remarry would have to say that both parties in a divorce could remarry without sin. A man could put away his wife for a cause other than fornication and remarry. She now puts him away "mentally" for fornication. She is free to remarry. He being the guilty party is also free to remarry without sin.

Arguments

(See the appendix for many more quibbles and arguments that are made to justify this position.)

1. "This puts the provision of civil law above God's law. If one who is put away unscripturally cannot then put away his adulterous mate (because he has already been put away), then the law of God is regulated by civil law."

This argument assumes a difference between divorce that is "real" and "legal" and that "marriage" and the "bond" are the same. We have already shown otherwise.

God's law states that "whoso marrieth her that is put away doth commit adultery" (Matt. 19:9b). Her being put away involves civil action. However, it is God's law that says she can't remarry.

All civil law does is ratify God's law. The position we have taken in this chapter does not put civil law above God's law, but merely respects it.

2. "In Matthew 5:32b and 19:9b — the 'her' refers not to any 'her,' but only to one where no fornication is involved as per verses 32a and 9a."

The point being made is that the one, who is put away without God's or his/her approval, and whose mate then commits adultery in remarrying, is not forbidden to remarry in the "b" part of these verses. If we were to grant that to be true, there is still no authority for any put away person to remarry. The text still says *"whoso marrieth her that is put away* doth commit adultery." There are no exceptions given. The one put away for fornication would be included for she is still bound. The one put away for a cause other than fornication is included (admitted by those who make the argument) for she is still bound. I don't know of any other put away one besides those two.

3. "The put away one who can remarry must be one who was against the divorce and opposed it. This eliminates the waiting game which is mutual agreement."

There is nothing in Matthew 5:32b or 19:9b that suggests that either party was opposed to the divorce or both mutually agreed to the divorce. This is an arbitrary rule. I wonder about a case where the couple mutually agree to a divorce, so he puts her away for a cause other than fornication. He then remarries, committing adultery. Can she not put him away mentally and remarry? What passage says she must have opposed the divorce?

4. "In Mark 10:10-11 when the man who unlawfully put away his wife remarries he commits adultery against her, thus giving her a scriptural cause to put him away."

This assumes that "against her" refers to the first wife. There is nothing that demands that interpretation. It is very possible that it refers to the second wife. "Another" (which refers to the second wife) is the nearest antecedent. Nigel Turner suggests that the word *epi* which is translated "against" has the meaning here of "with" (*The Bible Translator* [Oct. 1956], 151-152). Thus, when he remarries, he commits adultery with her (the second wife) (cf. Nestle's Text and The *Expositor's Greek Testament,* 1: 409).

I wonder if the woman of Mark 10:11 and the woman of Matthew 5:32b and 19:9b are not the same since the men of Mark 10:11 and Matthew 5:32a and 19:9a are. If so, then the woman of Mark 10:11 cannot remarry.

There is not a word in Mark 10:11 about remarriage on the part of a put away one. If we grant that "against her" refers to the first wife, so what? Neither this nor any other passage says one thing about her being able to remarry.

5. "Some societies have no legal ratification of marriage and no recognition of divorce."

This writer is not convinced that is so. Even if a couple divorce in a place where civil law does not come into play, there is still one who puts away and one who is put away. Matthew 19:9 can be observed whether society has any law concerning marriage and divorce or not. In a society that has such civil laws, they must be followed.

6. "You don't believe she can put him away (her husband who has unscripturally put her away and remarried) for fornication as Jesus said in Matthew 19:9."

If Jesus said she could, I would believe it. However, he didn't say one word about one who is put away then mentally putting her husband away and remarrying.

7. "It doesn't seem fair that this put away person (whose mate is adulterous) cannot put him away and remarry."

Go back and review Lesson 1 about the standard we shall use to determine what is right and wrong. Sometimes the innocent suffer from the sins of others (cf. Ezra 10:10, 11, 19, 44). Frankly, it doesn't seem any fairer that the penitent, guilty party who has been put away can't remarry. It neither seems fair that the woman put away for a cause other than fornication (whose husband doesn't remarry) should have to live a celibate life. Our standard must be the Bible and not our own reasoning.

Questions

Verses to remember: "For the woman which hath an husband is bound by the law to her husband so long as he liveth; but if the husband be dead, she is loosed from the law of her husband. So then if, while her husband liveth, she be married to another man, she shall be called an adulteress: but if her husband be dead, she is free from that law; so that she is no adulteress, though she be married to another man" (Rom. 7:2-3).

Discussion

1. Have someone in the class to explain the mental divorce position. _____

2. Discuss the "heart" (the bottom line) of this issue. _____

3. Discuss why the mental divorce advocates must confuse the *marriage* and the *bond*. _____

4. Discuss how this is an emotional issue and how such issues should be handled. _____

5. Discuss the consequences of the mental divorce position. _____

True or False

_____ 1. The "her" of Matthew 19:9b does not include the one put away (unscripturally) whose mate remarries.

_____ 2. If one is unscripturally married or divorced it is only in the eyes of man and not a real marriage or divorce in the eyes of God.

_____ 3. The whole issue here boils down to a race to the lawyer's office.

_____ 4. Mark 10:11 does not mention remarriage on the part of a put away one.

_____ 5. The "waiting game" is not a consequence of the mental divorce position.

Find the Passage

1. "And he saith unto them, Whosoever shall put away his wife, and marry another, committeth adultery against her." _____

2. "But and if she depart, let her remain unmarried, or be reconciled to her husband. ... " _____

3. "For the woman which hath an husband is bound by the law to her husband so long as he liveth ... So then if, while her husband liveth, she be married to another man . . ." _____

4. "For Herod himself had sent forth and laid hold upon John, and bound him in prison for Herodias' sake, his brother Philip's wife: for he had married her. For John had said unto Herod, It is not lawful for thee to have thy brother's wife." _____

5. "For it is evident that our Lord sprang out of Juda; of which tribe Moses spake nothing concerning priesthood." _____

Answer in a Few Words
1. Which put away one is it that some believe can remarry? _____
2. Cite three passages that show that, if a marriage or divorce is unscriptural, it is still a marriage or divorce. _____
   _____
3. How do we determine if the Bible uses accommodative language? _____
   _____
4. Which put away person does the Bible forbid to remarry? _____
5. How do you answer the charge that it is all a race to the lawyer's office if no put away person can remarry? _____
6. If the word "and" in the clause "and whoso marrieth her which is put away doth commit adultery" were to mean "or" as some contend, what would that verse mean? _____
   _____

Multiple Choice
_____ 1. Matthew 19:9b includes (a) only the one put away for fornication, (b) all put away people, (c) only the one put away for a cause other than fornication.
_____ 2. Bruce Metzger, Sakae Kubo, F. Wilbur Gingrich, and Zane Hodges said that the word "kai" translated "and" in Matthew 19:9 (a) could be translated "or," (b) must be translated "or," (c) could not be translated "or."
_____ 3. The clause "and whoso marrieth her which is put away . . ." found in Matthew 19:9 (a) has one exception, (b) has no exception, (c) has several exceptions.
_____ 4. Herod and Herodias were (a) not really married, (b) married with God's approval, (c) really married, though God disapproved.
_____ 5. The standard by which we determine right and wrong is (a) the Bible and it alone, (b) what seems fair and right to us, (c) the position of some well know preacher.

Fill in the Blank
1. The scriptural order of events in Matthew 19:9 is _____, _____ and _____.
2. The order that the mental divorce advocates have is _____, _____ and _____.
3. The _____ game is a consequence of the mental divorce position.
4. The mental divorce position confuses _____ and the _____. _____ is one passage that shows they are not the same.
5. There is no _____ for any put away one to remarry. We must respect the _____ of the Bible (cf. Heb. 7:14).

Lesson 9

Can the Guilty Party Remarry?

A verse to remember: *"Whosoever putteth away his wife, and marrieth another, committeth adultery: and whosoever marrieth her that is put away from her husband committeth adultery"* (Luke 16:18).

The body of Christ has been disturbed in some sections of the country (particularly the west coast) by those who advocate that the guilty party may scripturally remarry. This position is closely connected with the one in the previous lesson. Many brethren who hold this position also believe the one in Lesson 8. The consequences of the arguments made to justify the mental divorce position would lead the advocate to take the position under review in this lesson. One reason is that many of the arguments are the same.

The reader is encouraged to notice that the basic problem that this position has is the same problem that the mental divorce and other positions have, which is a failure to distinguish the *marriage* and the *bond*.

The Position Stated

This position focuses upon the guilty party rather than the innocent. It says that when there is a divorce for fornication that not only is the innocent free to remarry, but the guilty is also. The idea is that if the guilty is no longer married to the innocent, then he is free to remarry. The advocates of this position think that if one of the parties is *loosed*, both are *loosed*, thus allowing a scriptural remarriage.

To illustrate, if Jack puts Jill away because of fornication, then both of them are free to remarry.

There are some aspects of this position that are not accepted by some who believe that the guilty party can remarry. Some will tell us that fornication automatically severs the marriage (and the bond). Furthermore, it is argued that adultery is committed the first time one cohabits with another (other than his lawful mate). By this act the first marriage ceases to exist. Since there is no marriage, subsequent sexual acts are not adultery.

Cannot Remarry

1. Confusing the marriage and the bond. I encourage the reader to reread Lesson 5 which deals with the marriage and the bond in greater detail. The basic fallacy of the position, that says that the guilty party may remarry, is that it confuses the marriage and the bond. I have not read anything from any of the advocates of this position that indicates that they think the marriage and the bond are distinct. The concept is that marriage and the bond are the same. Thus, if a couple is no longer married, the husband and wife are no longer bound to each other. To be more specific, since the put away fornicator is no longer married, it is thought that he is no longer bound and is free to remarry.

Romans 7:2-3 demonstrates the difference in that the woman here was *bound* to her first husband even though she was *married* to another. This bond is the reason the second marriage is adulterous.

It is possible to be bound to one and married to another. Such is the case in Romans 7:2-3. The woman is "bound by the law to her husband" even though she is "married to another man." Matthew 19:9 says that the man who puts away his wife for fornication may scripturally marry another. Thus, he is *loosed*. But the one who marries the woman who is put away commits adultery. Thus, she is still *bound*.

God has loosed the innocent who has put away his mate for fornication. God has not loosed the guilty (Matt. 19:9).

2. Not authorized. Respect for the Lord and his authority causes us to understand that to act without authority is a sin (2 John 9). We cannot be presumptuous and think that God's silence is permission to act. Hebrews 7:14 demonstrates once for all time that God's silence is prohibitive (there is no authority), not permissive. Jesus could not be a priest on earth for he was of the tribe of Judah "of which tribe Moses spake nothing concerning priesthood."

God has authorized the innocent party to put away his/her mate for fornication and remarry (Matt. 5:32; 19:9). There is no passage that authorizes the put away fornicator to remarry. Matthew 5:32, 19:9, Mark 10:11-12, and Luke 16:18 do not grant such a right. Nor does any other passage provide the needed authority. To use human reasoning won't do. To say that no passage forbids it won't work. We must abide by the authority of Christ in this area as well as in the work, organization, and worship of the church.

3. Forbidden. Not only does God not authorize the guilty party to remarry, but he has forbidden it.

Jesus said that when the put away one remarries it is adultery. "... and whosoever shall marry her that is divorced committeth adultery" (Matt. 5:32b). "... and whoso marrieth her which is put away doth commit adultery" (Matt. 19:9b). "... and whosoever marrieth her that is put away from her husband committeth adultery" (Luke 16:18b).

Notice that there is no exception phrase in this clause that we just quoted. The exception in the first clause applies to the one who puts his mate away. Consider again chart 5.

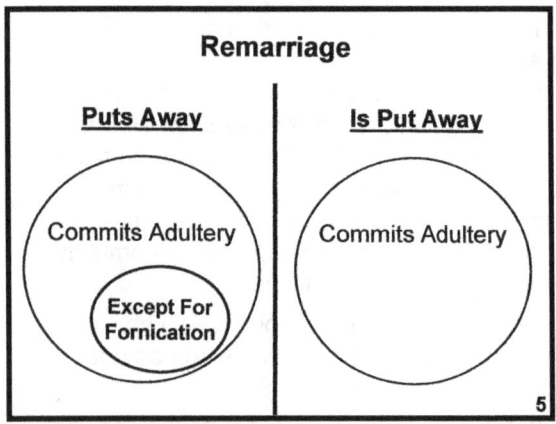

Obviously, when the put away one (whether for fornication or another reason) remarries, it is adultery. Consider chart number 7.

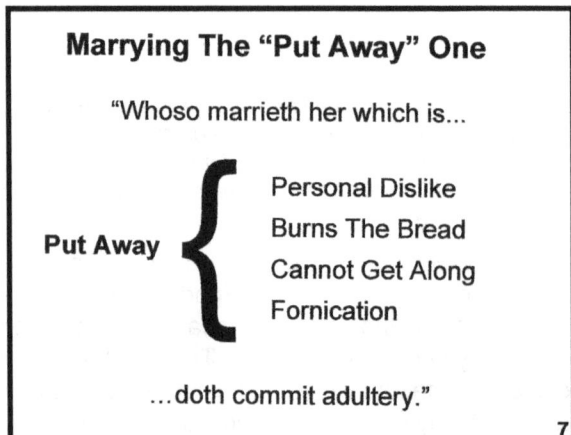

While it is not one hundred percent proof, the absence of a definite article ("the") before the put away woman in our text demonstrates that a particular put away woman is not under consideration, rather any put away woman.

Arguments

1. "If the put away fornicator cannot remarry without committing sin, then it would be a sin for him/her to be reconciled to his/her first mate."

The sin is in marrying another. The "whoso" (of Matt. 19:9) that marries the one put away is obviously someone other than the one who put her away. Reconciliation would be possible and scriptural, for the first mate would be the only one to whom the fornicator is bound. 1 Corinthians 7:10-11 shows that when the bond is still present reconciliation is the only course possible to have a scriptural marriage.

2. "If the innocent party is loosed, then the

guilty party is also loosed. When the bond is broken for one it is broken for the other. Just as two people tied together with a rope or handcuffed together, if one of the parties is freed, the other one is automatically."

The man and his wife are not the only elements in the bond. Romans 7:2-3 tells us that God's *law* (one mate for life) binds the two together. The two are bound *by* God's law to each other. One mate could be free while the other is still bound by the law. So, if we want to use the illustration of a rope or handcuffs, we would have the man and his wife tied or handcuffed together, but also to the law of God. Thus, if the man is untied (due to his wife's fornication) she is still tied by the law of God.

Maybe we can see it even clearer by the illustration of a yoke in chart 14. The man and woman were yoked together, but God could free one from the yoke and leave one in the yoke.

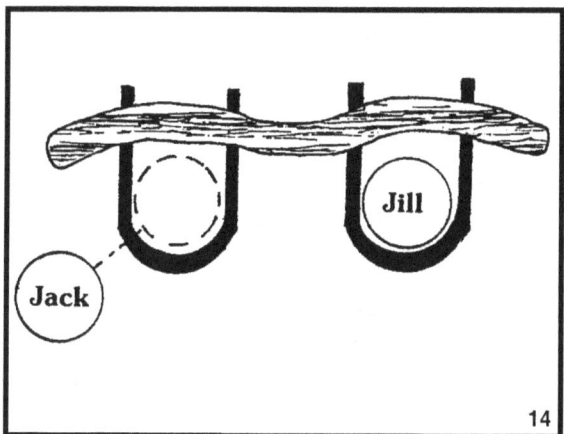

14

3. "Since the put away fornicator does not have a spouse, he is free to remarry because 1 Corinthians 7:2 says, 'Let every man have his own wife, and let every woman have her own husband.'"

Again, we see the confusion of the marriage and the bond. This assumes that if one is not married, he is not bound. We have previously shown that one could be unmarried (divorced) and still be bound. And if one is bound, he/she is not free to remarry.

Using the logic of this argument, one could justify the remarriage of one who has put away his mate unscripturally. Though Jesus said his marriage would be adultery (Matt. 19:9), I could reason that he doesn't have a wife, thus 1 Corinthians 7:2 says he has a right to marry one. The consequences of this type of reasoning is that there would be no unscriptural marriage. We could reason, if one is divorced, he doesn't have a wife, thus remarriage is scriptural.

4. "Where is the passage that places a penalty upon the guilty party?"

Matthew 5:32b and Matthew 19:9b state that adultery is committed when the put away one remarries. A better question would be, "Where is the passage that grants the put away fornicator the authority to remarry?"

5. "Matthew 19:9b ('and whoso marrieth her which is put away doth commit adultery') was added by a copyist. It is missing from some manuscripts. Therefore it is not a part of the original text."

Look back at Lesson 3 (section on textual problems) where the question about this clause is discussed.

6. "Adultery is committed by one who is married. Since the put away fornicator is not married, then it would not be adultery for him to remarry."

It is assumed that adultery is only committed by a married person. Jesus said that "whosoever" (whether he has been married or not) marries her that is put away commits adultery (Matt.

NOTES

5:32b; 19:9b; Luke 16:18b). Notice that he said that he (not she who has been married) commits adultery. Of course, she does too. Or is this text saying that it is adultery *only* if the man who marries her is a married man?

Walter Bauer says that the word "adultery" is used "2. of a man, who marries a divorced woman Mt 5:32b; 19:9 v.1 or who marries again after divorcing his wife 19:9..." *(A Greek-English Lexicon of the New Testament and Other Early Christian Literature,* 526).

Jesus used the word "adultery" in the very way that the above argument says it cannot be used. He said that a man who puts away his wife (thus not married) and marries another commits adultery (Matt. 19:9).

The same reasoning used in the argument above would justify a remarriage for one who is put away for a trivial cause. Such a person is not married and therefore could not commit adultery.

A careful look at Romans 7:2-3 will reveal that the reason a remarriage is *adultery* is because one is still *bound* to his first mate. When one is loosed from the law that binds him to his mate, there is no adultery if he chooses to remarry.

7. "The exception phrase in Matthew 19:9a also applies to the second clause ('and whoso marrieth her which is put away doth commit adultery')."

Look back to Lesson 4 (section on the exception phrase) where this is dealt with in detail.

8. "The 'her' in the clause, 'and whoso marrieth her which is put away ...' does not refer to the put away fornicator, but to one put away for another cause."

This same argument is dealt with in two different parts of Lesson 8 (sections on the put away one forbidden to remarry and arguments).

9. "Under the old covenant when a Jew put away his wife for a cause other than fornication, the effect was that both were free to remarry. In Matthew 19 Jesus didn't change the effect of the law on divorce and remarriage, only the number of causes."

Jesus also changed the effect. The adulterer under the old covenant was put to death (Lev. 20:10). Consider the points in Lesson 6 which show a clear contrast between the old law and Christ's law on marriage.

10. "The position advocated in this book would have two women bound to the same man. The put away fornicator and his new wife would be bound to him. If the bond involves obligation, then both are obligated to fulfill the requirements of 1 Corinthians 7:3-5 (due benevolence)."

The put away fornicator can no longer fulfill the requirements of 1 Corinthians 7:3-5, just as the one who must live a celibate life (1 Cor. 7:10-11). Sexual activity is to take place within marriage (Heb.13:4). The put away fornicator is no longer married.

Consider again Romans 7:3-4 which says that she is bound by the law to her husband.

11. "Fornication severs the marriage at the point it is committed, for God ordained that two are to be one and not three or more to be one. When the marriage is dissolved, the innocent is no longer married to the guilty and the guilty is no longer married to the innocent. Thus both are free to remarry."

Fornication is the *cause* and not the divorce itself. Jesus said that a man could put his wife away "*for* fornication." The fornication is committed before the divorce takes place. Otherwise, a man could commit fornication and his wife would be unmarried and not even know it. Thus, she unknowingly would be living with a man to whom she is not even married.

This argument confuses the *marriage* and the *bond*. It assumes that, if one is no longer married, he is no longer bound. We have already demonstrated otherwise.

12. "If the guilty party cannot remarry, then the innocent would have power over the life of the guilty to sentence him/her to celibacy."

No, God is the one who sentences the guilty to celibacy. Jesus said that anyone who marries the one who is put away commits adultery (Matt. 19:9). God simply gives the innocent the right to put away his mate who has committed adultery.

Consequences

1. If the put away fornicator can scripturally remarry, God's judgment is harder on the one *unjustly* put away than on the one *justly* put away.

2. Wife-swapping could be scriptural according to this position. To illustrate let's suppose we have two married couples in the local church: Jack and Jill, Tom and Jane. Jack commits fornication with Jane. Thus both are put away by Jill and Tom. All would agree that Tom and Jill could remarry. In this case they marry each other. Now, according to the doctrine under review in this chapter Jack and Jane could marry each other. Both couples could be accepted into fellowship.

Questions

A verse to remember: "And I say unto you, Whosoever shall put away his wife, except it be for fornication, and shall marry another, committeth adultery: and whoso marrieth her which is put away doth commit adultery" (Matt. 19:9).

Discussion

1. Discuss the basic points of the position under review in this chapter. _____
   _____

2. What is the basic fallacy of this position? _____
   _____

3. Discuss the two basic reasons why the put away fornicator cannot remarry. _____
   _____

4. What is the difference in the marriage and the bond? _____
   _____

5. How does this position confuse the marriage and the bond? _____
   _____

True or False

_____ 1. The Bible does not forbid the put away fornicator remarrying, only the one put away without a cause.

_____ 2. It is possible for one party in a marriage and divorce situation to be bound while the other is loosed.

_____ 3. The exception phrase applies to the last clause in Matthew 19:9 ("and whoso marrieth her which is put away...").

_____ 4. The "her" in "whoso marrieth her which is put away..." refers to any put away one.

_____ 5. The one who is unmarried (because of divorce) has a right to remarry.

Find the Passage

1. "But I say unto you, That whosoever shall put away his wife, saving for the cause of fornication, causeth her to commit adultery: and whosoever shall marry her that is divorced committeth adultery." _____

2. "For it is evident that our Lord sprang out of Juda; of which tribe Moses spake nothing concerning priesthood." _____

3. "For a woman which hath an husband is bound by the law to her husband so long as he liveth; but if the husband be dead, she is loosed from the law of her husband. So then if while her husband liveth, she be married to another man, she shall be called an adulteress . . ." _____

4. "Whosoever putteth away his wife, and marrieth another, committeth adultery: and whosoever marrieth her that is put away from her husband committeth adultery." _____

5. "And I say unto you, Whosoever shall put away his wife, except it be for fornication, and shall marry another, committeth adultery: and whoso marrieth her which is put away doth commit adultery." _____

Answer in a Few Words

1. What are the similarities and differences in the positions in lessons 8 and 9? _____

2. How is one loosed to remarry? _____

3. What is the difference in "divorced" and "loosed"? _____

4. What is the difference in "married" and "bound"? _____

5. How would you answer the argument that, if the innocent party is loosed then the guilty is also loosed, just as a couple tied together with a rope, if one is cut free, so is the other? _____

Multiple Choice

_____ 1. The put away fornicator (a) can scripturally remarry if he repents, (b) cannot scripturally remarry, (c) can remarry if his first mate were to commit adultery.

_____ 2. Adultery can be committed by (a) the married or the unmarried, (b) the unmarried only, (c) the married only.

_____ 3. When a couple divorce for fornication (a) both are still bound, (b) both are loosed, (c) one is loosed and one is bound.

_____ 4. The exception phrase applies (a) only to "b" part of Matthew 19:9, (b) only to part "a" of Matthew 19:9, (c) to both clauses.

_____ 5. (a) Matthew 19:9, (b) 1 Corinthians 7:27-28, (c) no passage, forbids the put away fornicator to remarry.

Fill in the Blank

1. Fornication does not _____ the marriage, but is the only scriptural _____ for a divorce.

2. The basic fallacy of this position is a confusion of the _____ and the _____.

3. The absence of a definite article ("the") from the last clause of Matthew 19:9 demonstrates that a _____ put away one is not under consideration.

4. The bond involves a _____ and his _____ and _____.

5. _____ _____ is one consequence of this position.

Lesson 10

1 Corinthians 7:15

A verse to remember: *"But if the unbelieving depart, let him depart. A brother or a sister is not under bondage in such cases: but God hath called us to peace" (1 Cor. 7:15).*

For many years brethren have discussed their differences on 1 Corinthians 7. To say the least, it is a difficult chapter. Numerous positions have developed from a misunderstanding of the chapter. Probably more has been said and written on this chapter and this verse (v. 15) than any other text in the discussion of divorce and remarriage.

The position dealt with in this chapter is basically the same as the one dealt with in chapter eleven. The major difference is that this lesson focuses on 1 Corinthians 7:15.

This discussion is a serious matter, for either the teaching of some on 1 Corinthians 7:15 will bring adulterers into the church or the teaching of others is shutting the door of the kingdom for them.

Credit must be given to Thomas B. Warren and Jerry Moffitt for some of the points made in this chapter.

The Position Stated

In this chapter we want to consider an abuse that is made of 1 Corinthians 7:15. Basically, the position says that the teaching of Christ on divorce and remarriage during his personal ministry (e.g. Matt. 19:9) is for those in a covenant relationship with God. Thus, we cannot apply that teaching to mixed marriages (a Christian married to a non-Christian) or to marriages of two non-Christians.

This position focuses on 1 Corinthians 7:10-15. We are told that 1 Corinthians 7:10-11 says that Christ in his personal ministry legislated on marriage, divorce, and remarriage for two Christians. We are told that verses 12-15 teach that Paul legislated on marriage, divorce, and remarriage for mixed marriages and that neither Paul nor Christ legislated on marriage, divorce, and remarriage for two non-Christians. Thus, passages such as Matthew 5:32 and Matthew 19:9 only apply to two Christians and do not apply to mixed marriages or marriages of unbelievers.

The conclusion would be that if a Christian divorced a Christian (for a cause other than fornication), they would still be bound, but if a non-Christian divorced a Christian for the same reason or a non-Christian divorces a non-Christian, they would not still be bound.

Much attention is given to "not under bondage" (v. 15). We are told that it refers to the bond of marriage and thus when the unbeliever leaves the believer, the bond of marriage is broken and the believer is free to remarry. To illustrate, let's suppose that *Jack* (a non-Christian) and *Jill* (a Christian) are married. Jack decides to divorce Jill for some reason other than fornication. The position under review would say that Jill is free from the marriage bond and thus free to remarry. The same would be true if they both were unbelievers.

This position would tell us that when we convert some non-Christian who has been divorced (for some cause other than fornication) and remarried that he/she would not be required to separate, but could continue in that marriage. The reason being that as long as they were unbelievers, they were not governed by the law of Christ on marriage. So, non-Christians and those in mixed marriages can divorce and remarry for any reason as frequently as they please. When they become Christians, they can keep their last mate and from then on they must abide by the teaching of Matthew 19:9.

All Men (Christians and Non-Christians) Are Amenable to the Law of Christ

We will deal with this section very briefly, in that Lesson 11 will focus greater attention on this point.

1. Under the law of Christ. All men (Christians and non-Christians) are subject to the law of Christ for the following reasons. (1)

Christ has all authority (Matt. 28:18). (2) The New Testament is addressed to all men (Matt. 28:18-20; Mark 16:15-16). (3) Those that reject Christ will be judged by the words of Christ (John 12:48).

If the non-Christian is not amenable to the law of Christ then we must conclude: (1) No non-Christian can obey the law of Christ. Thus, no one can be saved (2 Thess. 1:7-9). (2) No non-Christian sins when he enters a human denomination. (3) No non-Christian sins when he teaches a false doctrine, e.g. that baptism is not essential. (4) No non-Christian sins when he uses instrumental music in worship. (5) Since baptism is a part of the new covenant, then Christians, not non-Christians, are to be baptized. (6) What a non-Christian does to become a Christian is no part of the law of Christ (cf. Rom. 8:2). (7) No non-Christian sins when he urges people to reject the church that was purchased by the blood of Christ. (8) No non-Christian can be lost for disobeying the law of Christ. (9) No non-Christian has any obligation to worship in spirit and in truth. Thus, the non-Christian could use bacon and ice-cream for the Lord's supper and not sin in so doing.

2. Under Christ's law on marriage, divorce, and remarriage. If Christ's law on marriage doesn't apply to the alien, then no part of the gospel applies to the alien. Whoever is under the law of Christ is also under his law concerning marriage, divorce, and remarriage.

In Matthew 19:9 Jesus spoke of "whosoever" which includes all mankind. It includes all in Romans 10:13 and Acts 2:21.

If it is true that all men are subject to the law of Christ on marriage, divorce, and remarriage, then all who stand in violation of that law must sever that relationship to be forgiven (cf. 1 Cor. 5:1-13).

3. Confusing amenability with submission. Much that has been written on 1 Corinthians 7 has confused the concept of amenability with actual submission to the law. Statements like, "If all men are subject to the law of Christ, then all men would be Christians," have been made to suggest that all could not be amenable to the law of Christ. However, there is a difference between being amenable or subject to a law and actually obeying it. If we are going to confuse the two, why couldn't we say that any Christian who refuses to obey the law of Christ is not amenable to it?

1 Corinthians 7:15

1. The Context. Understanding the context of 1 Corinthians 7:15 has a great bearing on how one interprets that verse. The advocates of the position under review have had a lot to say about how the context says that Christ spoke only to two married Christians and that Paul spoke only about mixed marriages. Let's study the context and then the text.

a. Verses 10-11: (1) The instructions of these verses are addressed to the "married." Paul had addressed the "unmarried" in verses 8-9. Now he gives the instructions of the Lord for the "married." It is thought by some to be limited to two Christians who are married. Certainly, Christians are a part of the "married," but there isn't anything to indicate that it only applies to them. There is no justification for making "married" mean *some* of the married.

(2) It is possible that verses 10-11 refer to Matthew 19:9 and the parallel passages. I do know that he refers to some teaching during the personal ministry of the Lord for he says, "I command, yet not I, but the Lord." However, one would be hard pressed to prove that it does refer to Matthew 19:9 and not some unrecorded statement. One of the objections (that it isn't

Matt. 19:9) is that Matthew 19:9 doesn't say be reconciled or remain unmarried as 1 Corinthians 7:10-11 does. Yet, it could be countered that this is the conclusion to be drawn from Matthew 19:9.

(3) The instructions of these two verses are simple. They are (a) Don't divorce and (b) if you do, be reconciled or remain unmarried.

b. Verses 12-16.

(1) It is assumed by some that Paul makes a very important distinction by his use of the term "*rest*." We are told that since verses 12-16 address a situation where a believer is married to an unbeliever, then verses 10-11 must only apply to two believers. It is true that a distinction is made. However, it is more one of *issues* and *questions* than marriage types.

The *rest* may refer to those in a mixed marriage, as some commentators have suggested, but if so, Paul didn't really speak about the rest, for the marriage of two unbelievers is not dealt with. It is more reasonable to think that the "rest" refers to some additional matters (questions) they had asked the apostle Paul (cf. 1 Cor. 7:1). He answers those questions in verses 12-16.

(2) *"I, not the Lord"* is assumed to mean that the Lord's instructions of verses 10-11 (and Matt. 19:9) do not apply to mixed marriages. Nevertheless, the text does not say that the Lord didn't speak to unbelievers. Neither does the text say that those in mixed marriages and unbelievers are not under Christ's law on marriage.

If "I, not the Lord" means that Jesus said nothing about mixed marriages, then, "not I, but the Lord" (v. 10) must mean that Paul said nothing which applied to two married Christians.

All the text is saying is that Paul addresses some specific questions and issues about the marriage of a believer to an unbeliever which the Lord did not directly deal with in his personal ministry. We may safely infer from the nature of the questions being answered that they have to do with a situation wherein one mate has become a Christian (believer). The situation is quite different now than it was before for the Christian and the non-Christian. Thus, the Christian now has some questions about this marriage:

- Should a Christian man married to a non-Christian woman sever the relationship (v. 12)?
- Should a Christian woman married to a non-Christian man sever the relationship (v. 13)?
- Are Christians defiled by such a relationship, as they were in the Old Testament (v. 14)?
- Are children born to this relationship illegitimate (v. 14)?
- Is the Christian guilty of sin if the non-Christian leaves (vv. 15-16)?
- Does being a Christian mean that one must dissolve any marriage entered into before becoming a Christian (vv. 17-24)?

Jesus had not spoken specifically about the legitimacy of such marriages. That doesn't mean that his teaching in Matthew 19 does not apply to them. Neither had Jesus specifically addressed the questions of the marital status of virgins and widows during the present distress (cf. 1 Cor. 7:25-40), however the principles of Matthew 19:4-6 would include both of them.

(3) The instructions of these verses (and answers to the questions) can be summarized in three points. (1) The believer is not to depart from the unbeliever (vv. 12-13). (2) The marriage and the children are legitimate (v. 14). (3) If the unbeliever decides to depart, let him depart (vv. 15-16).

2. Verse 15.

a. "But if the unbelieving depart...." Why is the unbeliever leaving? It seems from the nature of the questions being answered that it must be a situation where one mate becomes a Christian and the unbelieving mate is placed in a situation of suffering along with the Christian during the present distress (vv. 26, 29), which was a short period of severe persecution. The unbeliever now finds himself married to one who has undergone a complete change. Thus, the believer is given an alternative: marriage or Christ! "Obviously, the reason for the unbeliever reacting this way is because of the faith of the believer, and the practice of that faith. It is not that the unbeliever just doesn't want to be married any longer; which could as well have been the case if two unbelievers were married" (Maurice Barnett, *Gospel Anchor*, Vol. X, No. 3 [Nov. 1983] 24).

If this passage justifies divorce and remarriage on the part of a believer married to an unbeliever, it would only be in a situation where the unbeliever left because of the faith of the believing mate.

If the unbeliever decides to depart, the believer is instructed to "let him depart." That expression does not sanction the departing at all. Consider some passages that have similar construction (1 Cor. 14:38; Rev. 22:11).

b. "Not under bondage...." (1) What is the bondage mentioned here? It is assumed by the defenders of the position under review that it refers to the bond of marriage as in Romans 7:2-3 and 1 Corinthians 7:27, 39. Others think it refers to the rule to stay with your mate and not depart (cf. vv. 10, 11, 12, 13). Another concept is that it refers to sin. That if the unbeliever leaves, the believer is not in the bondage of sin. Still others think it refers to marital responsibilities (cf. vv. 3-5). Thus, if your unbelieving mate leaves, you are not bound to fulfill those obligations. Another possibility is that it refers to being *enslaved* to your mate.

(2) It does not refer to the bond of marriage. The passages that obviously refer to the bond of marriage use the Greek word *deō* (Rom. 7:2-3; 1 Cor. 7:27, 39). However, in our text it is not the word *deō*, but *douloō*. If Paul was referring to the bond of marriage in verse 15, why didn't he use the word that he used twice in the same chapter to refer to it (vv. 27, 39)? *Douloō* is never used to refer to the bond of marriage. The word means slavery or enslavement. Consider the following quotations from the lexicons.

"to make a slave of, reduce to bondage" (*Thayer* 158).

"make someone a slave, ...enslave, subject" (*Bauer* 206).

"to enslave" (*Strongs* #1402).

"to enslave" (*Youngs* 103).

"enslave, subject" (*Kubo* 153).

"signifies to make a slave of, to bring into bondage" (*Vines* I:139).

"to be a slave ... to be a slave to another, be subject to, to serve, obey" (*Liddell and Scott* 179).

Thus, our text has reference to *enslavement*. The believer (in the situation described above) is not enslaved to the unbeliever to give up his/her faith to save the marriage. Thus, "let him depart."

(3) The tense of the word translated "not under bondage" suggests that he *has never been* under this bondage. Some have tried to infer that it must refer to the bond of marriage for that is the only bondage the believer has ever been under with reference to the unbeliever. However, this is the perfect tense in the Greek. "The Greek perfect tense denotes the present state resultant

upon a past action" (J. Gresham Machen, *New Testament Greek for Beginners,* 187). This means that the believer is not under bondage because he has never been under this bondage. Nestle's *Interlinear* translates it "has not been enslaved." One has never been enslaved to his mate to save the marriage at the expense of his faith.

(c) "In such cases...." This refers to the case where an unbeliever deserts the believer because of his faith. There is a contrast between verses 12-13 and verse 15. In the first, the unbeliever is content to dwell; thus, the believer is instructed to stay with his mate (vv. 12-13). In verse 15 the unbeliever is not content to dwell. In that case, the believer is instructed to let him depart.

3. Nothing is said about remarriage. Our text says nothing about the right of remarriage for the believer if the unbeliever departs. If justification can be found, it will be in another passage and not 1 Corinthians 7:15.

Arguments

The answer to many of these arguments will be found in the discussion of 1 Corinthians 7:15 and its context. Other arguments that are made to justify the position under review will be found in Lesson 11.

1. "The term 'whosoever' of Matthew 19:9 is limited for Paul said it applied to those in the covenant."

Paul didn't say that it only applied to those in a covenant relationship with God. What he said was that the Lord didn't address some questions that he (Paul) did address. This argument also assumes that 1 Corinthians 7:10-11 refers to Matthew 19:9.

2. "Paul plainly said that the Lord dealt with believers and not with mixed marriages (1 Cor. 7:10, 12)."

Again, this is based on assumption. The text doesn't say that the Lord's teaching did not apply to mixed marriages. To say that the Lord didn't address the questions being discussed in verses 12-16 does not mean that the Lord said nothing at all which applies to mixed marriages.

3. "'The rest' (1 Cor. 7:12) indicates that the Lord did not deal with mixed marriages, but Paul did."

We have already shown that "the rest" likely refers to the rest of the questions or issues being raised. Again, the text does not say that the Lord did not say anything that applied to mixed marriages.

4. "The prohibition of verse 11 is replaced by the liberty of verse 15."

Paul did not use the word "bound" in verses 10-11 as a contrast to "not under bondage" in verse 15. Remember that the nature of this bondage is that one has never been under it.

5. "God's people are different from the world: (a) The kingdom of God is not held up by a sword, the kingdoms of men are (Rom. 13). The church receives its money on a voluntary basis (1 Cor. 16:1-2), but the kingdoms of the world by taxation (Rom. 13). (c) The laws of pardon are different. (d) Believers are commanded to assemble (Heb. 10:25), partake of the Lord's supper (Luke 22:30), and disfellowship sinners (1 Cor. 5: 9-12)."

It is true that the kingdoms of the world and the kingdom of Christ are different. No one claims that the kingdom of Christ and the kingdoms of the world are the same. As we have pointed out earlier, some are confusing amenability and actual submission.

Furthermore, no one is amenable to a command that is not addressed to him. Certainly, there are commands addressed to Christians that are not addressed to aliens. No one person is qualified to obey every law in the gospel. For example, one cannot obey the requirements for the eldership and at the same time fulfill the duties of a wife. However, all can be required to obey the law of Christ!

6. "*Douloō* is derived from *deō* (Thayer 157-158) thus, the 'bondage' of 1 Corinthians 7:15 could refer to the bond of marriage."

What Thayer said was that *doulos* is "derived by most fr. *deō* to tie, bind; by some fr. *delō* to ensnare, capture. . ." (157-158). The fact that one word is derived from another doesn't mean that they are synonyms or that they mean the same. "Even if the two words do have a similar root, which is highly suspect, the test of explanation of words is their contexts" (William A. Heth and Gordan J. Wenham, *Jesus and Divorce,* 142).

7. "The alien sinner is in the same condition as the Gentiles were while the Old Covenant was in force. Neither are under God's law on marriage."

The Gentiles and aliens have always had a law on marriage, as well as all outsiders today. Gentiles during the Old Testament period were bound by Genesis 2:24. Gentiles today live under Matthew 19:9.

Consequences

Those who hold to the position that the alien sinner is not amenable to the law of Christ and that mixed marriages are not governed by Matthew 19:9 must face some serious consequences of their position.

1. A Christian could not marry another Christian who didn't fit the pattern of Matthew 19:9, but he could marry a non-Christian who didn't fit the pattern of Matthew 19:9 (i.e., one put away for fornication).

2. A non-Christian could live in a polygamous, group, homosexual, or incestuous marriage and not be sinning in so doing and could continue in that marriage after becoming a Christian.

3. There would be no marriage law which would apply to a non-Christian.

4. A Christian in a mixed marriage couldn't put away his unbelieving mate for fornication because Matthew 5:32 and 19:9 (the only passages that authorize it) only apply to two married Christians.

5. A Christian in a divorce situation would commit adultery only if he married another Christian. Thus, if one wanted to be free to divorce and remarry as he pleases he could simply keep marrying non-Christians.

6. If the Lord said *nothing* which applies to mixed marriages, then the following passages cannot apply to a mixed marriage:

- Leave father and mother (Matt. 19:5).
- Cleave to your mate (Matt. 19:5).
- The two are one flesh (Matt. 19:5).
- God hath joined them together (Matt. 19:6).
- Let no man put the marriage asunder (Matt. 19:6).
- Divorce for one cause (fornication) (Matt. 19:9).

Questions

Verses to remember: "But to the rest speak I, not the Lord: If any brother hath a wife that believeth not, and she be pleased to dwell with him, let him not put her away. And the woman which hath an husband that believeth not, and if he be pleased to dwell with her, let her not leave him" (1 Cor. 7:12-13).

Discussion

1. Discuss how the position under review explains 1 Corinthians 7:10-15. _____

2. Discuss whether or not 1 Corinthians 7:10-11 refers to Matthew 19:9. _____

3. Discuss the contrast between "not I, but the Lord" (v. 10) and "I, not the Lord" (v. 12). _____

4. Discuss the nature of the questions being answered in verses 12-16 and what that infers. _____

5. Discuss the consequences of the position that those in mixed marriages and aliens are not under the law of Christ. List any other consequences that are not listed in the lesson. _____

True or False

_____ 1. Christ did not teach anything that applies to mixed marriages.

_____ 2. "Bondage" in 1 Corinthians 7:15 is from the Greek word *deō* as in Romans 7:2-3 and 1 Corinthians 7:27, 39.

_____ 3. The "married" in verses 10-11 includes all who are married.

_____ 4. All who live in violation of Matthew 19:9 must sever that relationship to be forgiven.

_____ 5. 1 Corinthians 7:15 infers that remarriage is permissible.

Marriage, Divorce and Remarriage

Find the Passage
1. "And Jesus came and spake unto them, saying, All power is given unto me in heaven and in earth." _____
2. "But if the unbelieving depart, let him depart. A brother or a sister is not under bondage in such cases: but God hath called us to peace." _____
3. "He that rejecteth me, and receiveth not my words, hath one that judgeth him: the word that I have spoken, the same shall judge him in the last day." _____
4. "For the woman which hath an husband is bound by the law to her husband so long as he liveth; but if the husband be dead, she is loosed from the law of her husband. So then if, while her husband liveth, she be married to another man, she shall be called an adulteress . . ." _____
5. "The wife is bound by the law as long as her husband liveth; but if her husband be dead, she is at liberty to be married to whom she will; only in the Lord." _____

Answer in a Few Words
1. What does "bondage" (*douloō*) mean? _____
2. What is the point Paul is making in 1 Corinthians 7:12 by "I, not the Lord"? _____
3. Why is the unbeliever departing in 1 Corinthians 7:15? _____
4. What are the instructions to the married in 1 Corinthians 7:10-11? _____
5. What are the instructions to one in a mixed marriage in 1 Corinthians 7:12-16? _____

Multiple Choice
_____ 1. "Bondage" in 1 Corinthians 7:15 refers to (a) the bond of marriage, (b) the rule to stay with your mate (1 Cor. 7:10-13), (c) marital duties, (d) the bondage of sin, (e) enslavement.

_____ 2. The "rest" in 1 Corinthians 7:12 refers to (a) those not included in verses 10-11, (b) other questions or issues not dealt with by the Lord.

_____ 3. "Let him depart" in 1 Corinthians 7:15 (a) means that God approves of the departing, (b) does not sanction the departing, (c) means that the believer should encourage the unbeliever to depart.

_____ 4. In 1 Corinthians 7:15 the believer is (a) given permission to divorce his unbelieving mate, (b) given permission to remarry, (c) given instruction to let the unbeliever depart.

_____ 5. Unbelievers are (a) under Christ's law, (b) not under the law of Christ, (c) only under part of the law of Christ (e.g. the command to repent and be baptized).

Fill in the Blank
1. "Bondage" in 1 Corinthians 7:15 is from the Greek word _____ and not _____ that refers to the bond of marriage as in _____ and _____.
2. "Bondage" simply means _____. Thus, the believer is not _____ to the unbeliever to give up his _____ to save the _____.
3. All men are _____ to the law of Christ, for Jesus has all _____ (Matt. 28:18).
4. Those who hold the position under review in this chapter confuse _____ with actual _____.
5. The contrast between 1 Corinthians 7:10-11 and verses 12-16 is more one of _____ or _____ than _____ types.

Lesson 11

Does Matthew 19:9 Apply to Non-Christians?

A verse to remember: *"Because the law worketh wrath: for where no law is, there is no transgression" (Rom. 4:15).*

The question of whether aliens are amenable to the law of Christ on marriage has caused considerable trouble and concern. The interest increases as more and more Christians marry non-Christians. When divorce comes (no matter what the cause may be) some will immediately seek to find justification for remarriage. The question will continue to be discussed as long as men are speaking out in denial of the alien's amenability to Matthew 19:9 and as long as the process of divorce and remarriage continues.

This lesson is related to Lesson 10. Lesson 10 focuses on a specific argument made from 1 Corinthians 7:12-15. Lesson 11 focuses on the general question of whether Matthew 19:9 applies to the non-Christian.

The Position Stated

The position under review in this chapter is the same as the one in chapter 10. Some of our brethren are advocating that the law of Christ on marriage (Matt. 19:9) only applies to the marriage of two Christians. We are told that it does not apply to mixed marriages (a Christian married to a non-Christian). Nor does it apply to a marriage between two non-Christians.

Thus, those to whom Matthew 19:9 does not apply do not commit adultery when they do not abide by the principles found in the text.

Aliens Are Amenable to the Law of Christ

By "amenable" we mean accountable, answerable, or responsible to the law of Christ. It does not suggest that the alien in his present condition is obedient to the law of Christ. It simply suggests that he is subject or bound to keep the law of Christ.

1. All people are not answerable to all parts of the law. There are some laws that apply to parents. Thus, those who are not parents are not answerable to that part of the law of Christ. The same is true with reference to laws with specific application to elders, deacons, husbands, wives, children, servants, masters, churches, and individuals.

There are some parts of the law directed specifically to the alien sinner (e.g. baptism, Acts 2:38). There are some parts of the law directed specifically to the Christian (e.g. repentance and prayer for forgiveness, Acts 8:22; promises to hear one's prayer, 1 Pet. 3:12; 1 John 3:22).

2. Jesus Christ has universal authority. Jesus affirmed, "All power is given unto me in heaven and in earth" (Matt. 28:18). He has "power over all flesh" (John 17:2). He is the judge of the world (Acts 17:30-31), the Lord of all (Acts 10:36), and the prince of the kings of the earth (Rev. 1:5; see also Phil. 2:9-11; Rev. 19:16).

The authority that Jesus has is expressed through his word, for by it the world will be judged (John 12:46-48).

3. The world is subject to obey the law of Christ. The Great Commission was for the gospel to be preached to "all nations" or "every creature" (Matt. 28:18-19; Mark 16:15-16). That would include the alien and Christian alike. Furthermore, the judge of the earth will condemn all who do not obey his gospel (2 Thess. 1:8). The alien is required to obey the law of Christ in order to become a Christian (Rom. 8:2).

Follow carefully: (1) All men who violate the law of Christ are men who are subject to the law of Christ (Rom. 4:15). (2) Men in the world (aliens) are men who violate the law of Christ (Acts 17:23; Gal. 5:20; 1 Cor. 6:9-11). (3) Thus, we conclude, that aliens are subject to the law of Christ.

4. If one is amenable to part of the law, then he is amenable to all of the law (as a whole). Whether we are speaking of the Old Testament or the New, either one is a package deal (Gal. 5:3; Jas. 2:10). Thus, if the alien is subject to the part of the law that deals with faith, repentance, confession, and baptism (Rom. 8:2), then he is subject to the rest of the law of Christ.

This is not to imply that one subject to

the law is in a position to obey every single requirement of the law. That is true with civil as well as spiritual laws. In the state, there are laws that apply to the governor which do not apply to the legislator and vice-versa. Under the Old Testament there were laws that applied to the Levite which didn't apply to the rest. Under the New, there are laws that directly apply to elders which do not apply to the rest. There are commands that apply to wives which do not apply to the husbands and commands to husbands that do not apply to wives. Again, under the Old Covenant the requirement of circumcision was not bound upon all.

5. The alien is guilty of specific sins — all of which are violations of the law of Christ. Paul indicated that the alien in the world can be guilty of fornication, extortion, covetousness, and idolatry (1 Cor. 5:10). How could they be guilty of such sins as fornication or covetousness if they are not amenable to the law of Christ? Furthermore, the Corinthians had been guilty of the above list and more before they became Christians (1 Cor. 6:9-11). How could they have been guilty of adultery if they were under no law on marriage?

6. How did the alien become a sinner in the first place? If the alien is not amenable to the law of Christ, how did he become a sinner? Remember, that sin is a transgression of the *law* (1 John 3:4). And, where no law is, there is no transgression and thus no sin (Rom. 4:15)!

God Has One Body of Laws for the Christian and Alien

God doesn't have one set of laws for the Christian and another set of laws for the alien. The body of laws he has given to one is the same that he has given to another.

1. The laws are directed to both Christians and aliens. (1) The *gospel* is for the alien (Mark 16:15) and the Christian (Rom. 1:7, 15; Gal. 2:14). (2) The *doctrine* is addressed to the alien (Acts 5:28; John 6:44-45) as well as the Christian (Acts 2:42; 2 John 9). (3) The *word* is presented to the alien (Acts 13:5-7) and the Christian (2 Tim. 4:2). (4) The *faith* was delivered to the alien (Acts 6:7) as well as the Christian (Jude 3). (5) The *truth* is applicable to the alien (John 8:32) and the Christian alike (Gal. 2:5).

2. The gospel is the word and truth. Whether you call it the gospel, doctrine, word, faith, or truth, they all refer to one and the same body of laws. Paul demonstrated this when he wrote, "For the hope which is laid up for you in heaven, whereof ye heard before in the *word* of the *truth* of the *gospel*" (Col. 1:5, emphasis mine, DVR). The gospel and doctrine are the same, for what Romans 6:17 calls obeying the form of *doctrine*, Romans 10:16 calls it obeying the *gospel*.

What Law Is the Alien Under?

1. Civil law alone? Some have argued that the alien is not under the law of Christ, but is only under civil law. However, aliens were commanded to repent of idolatry (Acts 17) which is not a violation of civil law, but of the law of Christ (Gal. 5:20). The Corinthians had been guilty of covetousness when they were aliens (1 Cor. 6:9-11). What civil law condemns covetousness?

2. Law in the heart? Some have contended from Romans 2:13-15 that there is a mysterious "law in the heart" under which were the Gentiles and all aliens today. Men become sinners by violating the "law in the heart" we are told.

a. What is this "law in the heart"? Where can we read it? How can we know what is in it?

Those who tell us about this law don't seem to know any more about it than we do.

b. In Romans 2 it was the "works" of the law and not the law itself which was written in the heart. "The construction of the Greek shows plainly that it was the work of the law, and not the law itself, that was written on the hearts of the Gentiles" (Robertson L. Whiteside, *A New Commentary on Paul's Letter to the Saints at Rome,* 58). Notice that in verse 15 Paul said, "Which show the *work* of the law written in their hearts . . ." (emphasis mine, DVR). In verse 26 he speaks of the uncircumcision (Gentiles) keeping the righteousness of the law.

Thus, the law referred to in Romans 2:13-15 was the law of Moses and not some mysterious law. The context shows that it was the law that the Gentiles did not have (vv. 12-15).[1]

c. Though the law of Moses was not given to the Gentiles, they had adopted some of those moral principles that were found in it. Thus, they had the law written in their hearts. They were guided by what their nature prompted them to do and thus became a law unto themselves.

3. All are under Genesis 2:24 (God's law on marriage). In the very beginning God stated his law, "Therefore shall a man leave his father and his mother, and shall cleave unto his wife: and they shall be one flesh" (Gen. 2:24). Though the law of Moses was given to the Jews, it did not change the condition of the rest of the world which were already under God's law in the beginning.

When Jesus states concerning divorce, "from the beginning it was not so" (Matt. 19:8), he uses the present perfect which suggests that it was true in the past and continues to the present.

Jesus' teaching in Matthew 19:9 fully agrees with Genesis 2:24.

The Nature of a Covenant

1. An agreement between two parties? The concept of many is that the word "covenant" suggests that there is an agreement between two or more parties. The conclusion made by some is that since the alien has not agreed to a covenant, he is not amenable or subject to the requirements of God's covenant. Let us look more closely at the word and how it is used in the Bible.

2. Defining the word. The English word "covenant" comes from the Greek word *diathēkē*. It does not suggest that there must be an agreement before there is a covenant. (1) *Vine* says it "primarily signifies a disposition of property by will or otherwise... . In contradistinction to the English word 'covenant' (lit., a coming together), which signifies a mutual undertaking between two parties or more, each binding himself to fulfill obligations, it does not in itself contain the idea of joint obligation, it mostly signifies an obligation undertaken by a single person. For instance, in Gal. 3:17 it is used as an alternative to a 'promise' (vv. 16, 17 and 18). God enjoined upon Abraham the rite of circumcision, but His promise to Abraham, here called a covenant, was not conditional upon the observance of circumcision, though a penalty attached to its non-observance" (*Expository Dictionary of New Testament Words* I: 250-251). (2) *Moulton and Milligan* say, "*Diathēkē* is properly *dispositio*, an 'arrangement' made by one party with plenary power, which the other party may accept or reject, but cannot alter" (J.H. Moulton and G. Milligan, *The Vocabulary of the Greek Testament,* 148; also quoted in the

---

[1] For more see my tract entitled "The Gentiles and the Law of the Conscience."

Theological Dictionary of the New Testament, Gerhard Kittel, editor, II: 125).

3. Biblical examples. There are a number of cases where God referred to a command, promise or law as a covenant. Notice that in each of these, it was a covenant whether or not man agreed to it.

  a. Genesis 9:8-17 calls God's promise not to destroy the earth by a flood a covenant.

  b. Genesis 17:2-8 uses the term covenant to refer to God's promise to Abraham to multiply his seed and make nations of him. This was also a covenant with the seed of Abraham not yet born!

  c. The Ten Commandments are called a covenant (Exod. 19:5; 34:27-28; Deut. 4:13; Heb. 9:4).

  d. God uses the terms "law" and "covenant" interchangeably (Jer. 31:33; Heb. 10:16).

  e. Joshua 24:25 shows that a covenant is a statute and ordinance.

  f. A covenant is a command (Josh. 23:16).

If it be true that a covenant always involves an agreement between two parties, I wonder if the Jews were answerable to God's covenant on the Sabbath only after they agreed to keep it. Numbers 15:32-36 clearly shows otherwise.

4. Don't confuse enjoying the privileges of a covenant with being accountable to a covenant. The former is dependent upon obedience to the covenant, the latter is not.

Matthew 19:9

This clear and simple passage which states the law of Christ with reference to divorce and remarriage applies to the alien as well as the Christian.

1. It was not addressed to Christians. The truth of Matthew 19 was spoken to "great multitudes" (Matt. 19:2-3). The question about divorce was asked by the Pharisees (v. 3), whose motive was to tempt the Lord. He addressed his answer (vv. 4-12) to an audience that did not contain one single Christian. Though verse 9 seems to be parallel with Mark 10:10 (spoken to the disciples in the house), the point is still the same.

2. Jesus applied his law on divorce and remarriage to "whosoever" (Matt. 19:9; 5:32). "Whosoever" is universal (cf. Rom. 10:11, 13; Rev. 22:17).

3. The law (of which Matt. 19:9 is a part) is addressed to every creature (Matt. 28; Mark 16).

4. The context of Matthew 5:32. The context of Matthew 5:32 lists a number of sins that are just as wrong for the non-Christian as they are for the Christian. The warnings about (1) murder (v. 21), (2) anger (v. 22), and (3) adultery (vv. 27-28) apply to the alien as well as the Christian. Likewise, verse 32 applies to both.

Arguments

1. "God doesn't join aliens together in marriage."

Herodias and Philip were both aliens and were said to be married (Mark 6:17-18). Marriage is not a "church" ordinance, but a thing God established in the very beginning (Gen. 2:24).

2. "Those who are aliens are 'free from righteousness' (Rom. 6:20), thus not accountable to the law of God."

The consequence of this kind of reasoning is that as long as men are in sin they are not accountable to *any* law of God, even the one on baptism! The actual point in the text is that as long as men are in sin they are not righteous.

3. "When the gospel speaks to outsiders

and tells them what to do to come into the covenant, it does not mean that while outside the covenant they are obligated to observe all the commands of the covenant. For example the Old Covenant gave instructions to come into the covenant, but those without (Gentiles) were not obligated to obey the laws of the covenant. Likewise, those laws spoken to those outside the covenant are not directed to those within."

We must remember that while the Old Covenant was directed to the Jews, the New Testament is addressed to *all men* (Matt. 28; Mark 16). Again, that doesn't mean that every person is accountable to every law. We must also remember that the Gentiles always had a law on marriage as well as all aliens (Gen. 2:24).

4. "The alien is not to partake of the Lord's supper thus, the alien is not under the law of Christ."

Using that same reasoning one could say, "Since the unbeliever is not to be baptized, the unbeliever is not subject to the first principles of the gospel." No one out of the church could be baptized since all at one time are unbelievers. The above argument would be tantamount to saying that since the state law requiring a driver's license does not apply to the person riding a bike, he therefore is not under any state law. Let us not forget that the Lord's supper is specifically for those in the kingdom (Matt. 26:29; Luke 22:18-19).

5. "The law of Christ is not retroactive. There is no command or example demanding the breakup of a marriage of those who have become Christians."

The law of Christ doesn't have to be retroactive to demand a breakup. We have already noticed that the law of Christ on marriage (Matt. 19) was in harmony with God's law from the beginning (Gen. 2:24). All have been under that law all along.

If the law of Christ doesn't demand any kind of a breakup, I wonder about those in an incestuous marriage or homosexual or polygamous marriage. Could they continue in their relationships?

6. "The law is not addressed to all, but only to those that are under it (Rom. 3:19-20)."

The Old Law spoke to the Jews, for it was addressed to the Jews and not the Gentiles. However, the New Testament is addressed to all men (Matt. 28; Mark 16), thus it speaks to all. All are amenable to it, though all do not obey it.

7. "The non-Christian is convicted of sin by the 'law in the heart' (Rom. 2) and not the law of Christ."

The law written on the heart does not forbid denominationalism, instrumental music, or rejecting the plan of salvation or the church. Is it not a sin to be guilty of these? See the previous section in this chapter about the "law in the heart."

8. "The new law was directed to spiritual Israel (Jer. 31:31-34; Heb. 8), thus it is for those who are the people of God. It was delivered to the saints (Jude 3)."

While all of the above is true, let us not forget the simple fact that the gospel is addressed to all men (Matt. 28; Mark 16).

9. "Paul spoke of the Jews as being under the law and the Gentiles as being without law (1 Cor. 9:20-21). Thus the alien, like the Gentile, is without law."

The point of this text is that the apostle Paul could accommodate himself to the customs and practices of the Jews or Gentiles in an effort to reach them. When among Jews, he lived like a Jew (though not binding the law of Moses upon himself or others). When among the Gentiles, he did not practice the customs of the Jews. Lest any misunderstand, Paul adds that he is under the law of Christ.

Keep in mind that, if the passage is saying that the Gentiles and the alien are not under any law, then they could not be under the law in the heart. Also, if they are not under any law, they could not be guilty of sin (1 John 3:4).

As Paul writes this letter, the Jews were not under the law of Moses for it had already been abolished (Col. 2:14). They were only "under the law" in that they regarded themselves as still being under that law.

10. "God had all authority in the Old Testament, but not all were under his covenant. Likewise, under the New Testament Christ has all authority, but not all are subject to him."

It is true that not all obey Christ. However, that doesn't mean that all are not amenable to him. There is a difference in the Old and New Testaments. The old law was to the Jews, whereas the new is for all men (Matt. 28; Mark 16).

11. "Those with a carnal mind are not subject to the law of God (Rom. 8:7)."

Is it possible for a Christian to have a carnal mind? If so, then no Christian is amenable to the law of Christ according to the argument. The word "subject" in this text does not mean "accountable," but it means to be obedient (*Thayer*, 645). See how the same word (in English and Greek) is used in Romans 13:1.

12. "Only the citizens of the United Kingdom are subject to their king. Those in another kingdom are not subject. Likewise those outside the kingdom of Christ are not subject to him."

This assumes that Christ only has authority in his kingdom. Matthew 28:18-19 demonstrates that he has all authority. The analogy will not work in that it doesn't agree in all parts. Furthermore, any who serve in the dominion of Satan are in rebellion to Christ (Jas. 4:4; Eph. 2:2-3).

13. "The citizens of Great Britain are not under American law when they are taking necessary steps of 'naturalization' to become citizens of America. Likewise, the alien, who must obey the first principles to become a Christian is not under the law of Christ."

The terms of entrance into the kingdom of Christ are part of the law of Christ (Rom. 8:2). The illustration above is not parallel at all, for the United States does not have a law ("gospel") that if anyone rejects it he will be damned, yet the Lord does have such a gospel (2 Thess. 1:7-9).

If a Briton should visit our country and murder someone while here, he would be violating American law.

14. "If Christ rules over the world and his church, then he rules over two bodies."

Again, let us not confuse being amenable with being a part of the kingdom. While the whole world is amenable to the law of Christ, only a few are in his one body. Let us ask if the denominationalist sins when he uses instrumental music? If so, does that mean there must be two kingdoms or bodies?

Consequences

As pointed out in the previous chapter, those that hold to the position under review must face some very serious consequences of their position. They are:

1. As long as one remains in rebellion to the Lord, he is not accountable. But, as soon as he

submits to the Lord, he is now amenable to the law of Christ and can no longer do the things he did. Before, they were not sin. Now they are.

2. No one is obligated to obey the gospel (faith, repentance, confession, and baptism) since these things are a part of the law of Christ.

3. The denominationalists do not sin when they use the instrument of music.

4. Baptism would be for the Christian since only the Christian is amenable to the law of Christ.

5. If we can preach to the alien and yet he is not subject to the law of Christ, there must be a distinction between *gospel* and *doctrine* as the new-unity/grace-fellowship brethren have argued.

6. If the alien is not subject to the law of Christ, then the very mission of the church and work of gospel preachers are cast aside.

NOTES

Questions

Verses to remember: "And Jesus came and spake unto them, saying, All power is given unto me in heaven and in earth. Go ye therefore, and teach all nations, baptizing them in the name of the Father, and of the Son, and of the Holy Ghost" (Matt. 28:18-19).

Discussion

1. Discuss the meaning of the word "covenant." _____
   _____

2. Discuss the difference in being "amenable" and being "obedient." _____
   _____

3. Discuss the consequences of the position under review. _____
   _____

4. Discuss the different senses in which the term "subject" is used. _____
   _____

5. Discuss the different ideas about what law the alien is under. _____
   _____

True or False

_____ 1. A covenant always involves an agreement between two parties.

_____ 2. Jesus has all authority (over the Christian and alien alike).

_____ 3. Matthew 19:9 was spoken to a group of Christians.

_____ 4. If one is not under the law of Christ, he is not guilty of sin.

_____ 5. If the alien is subject to the law of Christ, he must observe the Lord's supper.

Find the Passage

1. "For the hope which is laid up for you in heaven, whereof ye heard before in the word of the truth of the gospel." _____

2. "Because the law worketh wrath: for where no law is, there is no transgression." _____

3. "All power is given unto me in heaven and in earth." _____

4. "And I say unto you, Whosoever shall put away his wife, except it be for fornication, and shall marry another, committeth adultery:, and whoso marrieth her which is put away doth commit adultery." _____

5. "Go ye into all the world, and preach the gospel to every creature." _____

6. "Go ye therefore, and teach all nations, baptizing them...." _____

Answer in a Few Words

1. What does "amenable" mean? _____
2. What does "covenant" mean? Give some Bible passages as examples. _____
   _____
3. How do you know that all men (Christians and aliens) are amenable to the law of Christ? _____
   _____
4. What is the "law in the heart"? _____
   _____
5. Give evidence that Matthew 19:9 applies to all. _____
   _____

Multiple Choice

_____ 1. Matthew 19:9 was addressed to (a) Christians, (b) great multitudes.

_____ 2. A covenant (a) is always an agreement between two parties, (b) can be a command or a promise, (c) is only for those who are Christians.

_____ 3. The gospel is (a) only to the alien, (b) only to the Christian, (c) to both the alien and the Christian.

_____ 4. The "gospel" (a) is only the first principles, (b) does not include the Lord's teaching on marriage, (c) is the same as the word and the truth.

_____ 5. Aliens, like the Gentiles of old, have always been under (a) civil law alone, (b) the law in the heart, (c) Gen. 2:24.

Fill in the Blank

1. If the alien is not under the _____ of Christ, he could not be guilty of _____, for sin is a transgression of _____.
2. Jesus has _____ authority.
3. Romans 2 shows that it was the _____ of the law and not the law itself that was written in the heart.
4. By "amenable" we mean _____, _____ or _____ to the law of Christ.
5. The gospel is the _____ of the _____ (Col. 1:5).

Lesson 12

Must Adulterers Separate? Or, Are Adulterous Marriages Washed Away at Baptism?

Verses to remember: *"And the times of this ignorance God winked at; but now commandeth all men every where to repent: because he hath appointed a day, in the which he will judge the world in righteousness by that man whom he hath ordained; whereof he hath given assurance unto all men, in that he hath raised him from the dead" (Acts 17:30-31).*

The previous lessons have dealt with who can and cannot scripturally marry and to whom God's law applies. This lesson deals with the question of what must be done with those in adulterous marriages. With the increase of divorce and remarriage among God's people has come the question of what we do about those who are in adultery.

Suppose for a moment that a couple wants to be baptized, and you find out that it is the third marriage for him and the fourth for her (all unscriptural). What must they do? Does the Bible demand that they separate or can they continue in that same marriage? Or, suppose that two Christians who obtained unscriptural divorces from their first mates marry each other. When they finally realize that they have sinned and want forgiveness, what must they do? Must they separate or can they continue in that marriage? These questions will be addressed in this lesson.

The Position Stated

There are two basic views that say that no separation is required of those being baptized. (1) One says that the alien is not under the law of Christ and thus has not violated any of his teaching on marriage. Those who hold this position would not talk about "adulterers" needing to separate for they do not believe that it would be adultery for the alien to divorce (for a cause other than fornication) and remarry. The idea is that when one is baptized he then enters a covenant relationship with God and is now accountable to God's law on marriage. Thus, no separation of a previous marriage is necessary. (2) The other idea says that the alien is under the law of Christ, and does commit adultery if he remarries following an unscriptural divorce. However, separation is still not required for baptism will wash away the sin and they can continue in that marriage.

Some make a similar application to Christians who are in an unscriptural marriage and decide to repent. They argue that repentance does not demand that they separate.

This writer affirms that in both cases (alien and the Christian) the adulterers must separate.

The real point in question is what repentance demands. Our second point of focus will be on the nature of adultery.

Repentance

1. It is required. Forgiveness of sin is conditioned upon repentance. It is required for the alien sinner (Acts 2:38; 17:30-31) and the erring child of God (Acts 8:22).

2. Defined. A very simplistic definition of repentance is a change of mind. However, repentance involves (or at least produces) a change in life: *ceasing the past sin!* This definition will be seen from two sources:

a. The Greek authorities: The Greek word translated "repentance" means "to change one's mind for the better, heartily to amend with abhorrence of one's past sins" (Thayer, 405). W.E. Vine says "this change of mind involves both a turning from sin and a turning to God" (III: 281). Kittel's *Theological Dictionary of the New Testament* suggests that repentance involves turning away from evil (IV: 1004). A.T. Robertson said that when John called upon his hearers to repent, "John did not call on people to be sorry, but to change their mental attitudes and conduct" (*Word Pictures in the New Testament,* I: 24).

b. Bible passages: John preached, "Bring forth fruits meet for repentance" (Matt. 3:8). Repentance has fruits. Compare Matthew 12:41 and Jonah 3:10. What Matthew 12:41 calls *repentance,* Jonah 3:10 describes as *turning from evil.* Though it uses a different Greek word, Matthew 21:28-29 demonstrates that repentance involves a change of mind and a change of action; for the son, who refused to work, repented and "went."

3. The point is the act of sin must cease! This is true of any sin, whether it be the sin of idolatry or the sin of adultery. Consider the illustration in chart 22.

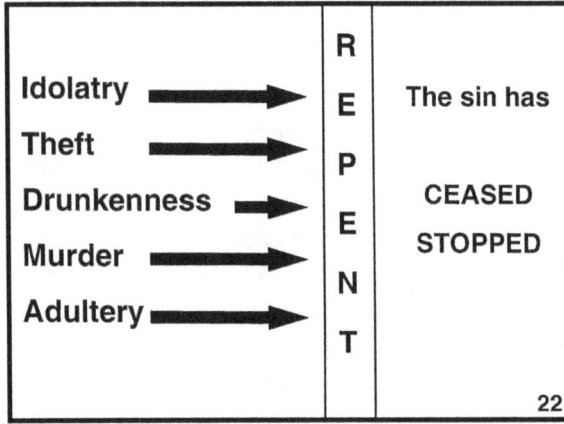

22

If one does not stop or cease the sin, then there has been no repentance. Revelation 9:20-21 describes some who didn't change and continued on in their sins as having "repented not." Read 2 Corinthians 12:20-21 carefully and you will see that Paul was concerned about some who had not stopped or ceased their sin, but continued in their former practice. Notice that he refers to them as those who "have not repented." Thus, if the practice continues there has been no repentance. Consider the illustration in chart 23.

The crux of the issue is not *restitution* or *undoing* the past (as some have argued), but it is *ceasing* the sin.

Adultery

1. Defined. The Greek word translated "adultery" means "to have unlawful intercourse with another's wife" (Thayer, 417). This is a more specific term than fornication, at least as it is generally used. Look back to Lesson 2 for more information.

2. A misconception about adultery is that it simply means "covenant breaking" or "breaking wedlock." The concept is that the unscriptural divorce and remarriage (thus breaking the covenant of the first marriage) constitutes adultery and not the unlawful sexual activity. When the couple decides to repent, they repent of the divorce and remarriage and quit divorcing and remarrying. However, they can continue in that marriage (and sexual relations) without it being adultery, we are told.

The term "adultery" is not used that way in the Bible. Jesus said that a man who looks upon a woman and lusts after her has committed adultery in his heart (Matt. 5:28). Was he fantasizing about breaking the covenant or sexual relations? In John 8 the Pharisees brought a woman to Jesus, whom they said was caught in the "very act" of adultery (v. 4). Was she caught in the act of divorcing and remarrying (breaking wedlock) or in the sexual act? Ezekiel 16 tells the parable of the unfaithful wife. What verse 32 calls *adultery* the context calls "fornication" (v. 15) and harlotry (vv.15-16) and "whoredom" (vv. 25-26) and taking "strangers instead of her husband" (v. 32).

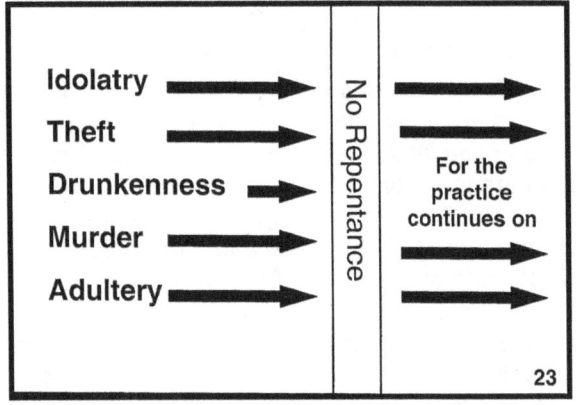

23

In Matthew 5:32 we see that the woman who is put away (for a cause other than fornication) commits adultery when she remarries. Was she the one who broke the covenant (by getting the unscriptural divorce)? No, her husband did. But she is still guilty of adultery when she remarries (cf. Walter Bauer, *A Greek English Lexicon of the New Testament and Other Early Christian Literature* 526).

Furthermore, there is *no lexicon* or *passage* that would justify this arbitrary definition of adultery as "covenant breaking."

3. Another misconception is that one can't "live in adultery," but that adultery is committed the first time the couple cohabits (thus dissolving the first marriage). All subsequent sexual acts are not adultery. Again, when the couple decides to repent, they simply repent of having broken up the first marriage and the first sexual act, but can continue in their relationship.

The Greek word translated "committeth adultery" (*moichatai*) is in the present tense which denotes continuous action. The adultery is committed as long as they continue to cohabit. "The present tense indicates *progressive* action at the present time..." (Ray Summers, *Essentials of New Testament Greek*, 11). "Continued action, or a state of incompletion, is denoted by the present tense, — this kind of action is called durative or linear" (William Hersey Davis, *Beginner's Grammar of the Greek New Testament*, 25). For a parallel consider the word "believeth" (John 11:26) which is also present tense. Does it refer to the initial act of faith or a progressive faith?

For more evidence that the present tense denotes continuous action, reread the section on adultery in Lesson 2.

Colossians 3:5-7 clearly shows that one can "live in adultery." Verse 5 enumerates some sins which must be put to death. Among them is the sin of *fornication*. Then, verse 7 says that the Colossians had one time "lived in them." They had lived in fornication, the very thing that some brethren say cannot be done. Romans 7:2-3 shows that a woman who marries another man would be called an adulteress as long as her first husband lives. Without question people can and do live in adultery.

4. If an act is adultery before repentance, then that same act is adultery after repentance (and baptism). If not, then the Christian is released from obligation to the law of God. A marriage is either scriptural or unscriptural. If it is *unscriptural* before repentance and baptism, then being baptized does not change a thing about that marriage. That same marriage is still *unscriptural*.

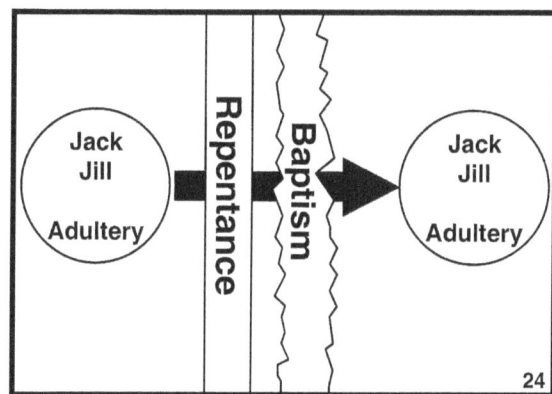

Does Baptism Wash It All Away?

The concept of a few of our brethren is that the sin of adultery is washed away at baptism and thus the couple can continue in their present marriage without further sin.

It is true that sin is washed away when one is baptized (Acts 2:38; 22:16). However, baptism does not change an unlawful deed into a lawful one. Whether it be the sin of adultery or the sin of polygamy, the sin must stop before baptism will wash away the guilt. If the adulterer can continue in his marriage following baptism (and be forgiven), then so can the polygamist continue with his six wives. Consider chart 25.

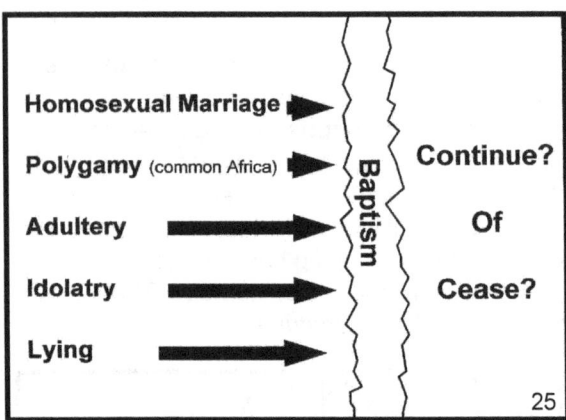

Arguments

1. "All sin is washed away in baptism, including adultery."

It is true that all sin is washed away in baptism, but that is conditioned upon repentance which involves ceasing the sin. Remember, what works for the adulterer will also work for the homosexual and the polygamist.

2. "There is no command, example, or necessary inference in the Bible demanding the separation of adulterers."

Every passage that commands repentance is a passage that commands adulterers to separate. Colossians 3:5 is a *command* to mortify (put to death or cease) sinning. One of the sins mentioned specifically is fornication. Colossians 3:7 is an *example* of the Colossians having put away their fornication. In that Matthew 19:9 tells us that they continue to live in adultery as long as they cohabit, it *necessarily infers* that they must separate. The case of Herod and Herodias is another example of a couple being told they must separate (Mark 6:17-18).

Those who make this argument must be careful for one could argue on the same basis that there is no command, example, or necessary inference that tells the homosexual or the polygamist to separate.

3. "Those converted on the day of Pentecost (Acts 2) were not told they had to separate."

If that proves anything, it proves that no homosexual or polygamist must separate because one doesn't read anything about them being told to separate in Acts 2. Don't forget though, they were told to repent (v. 38).

4. "You can't go back and undo some sins of the past, for example: murder."

Murder is not really parallel with the sin of adultery for you can "undo" the marriage. The question is not undoing the past, but *ceasing* the sin. Shall we tell the polygamist and the homosexual that their sin is like murder, that he can't go back and undo it?

5. "To ask a happily married couple to separate seems so unfair and unjust especially where there are children involved."

This contention is based upon emotion rather than Scripture (cf. Lesson 1). When God's people married the strangers of the land after they returned from captivity, Ezra stood up and demanded that they separate (Ezra 10:9-10). Was that fair? Was that just? Are we to set in judgment on God and suggest that Ezra's instruction was too harsh and cold? And, by the way, there were children involved (v. 44). Was John unfair and unjust in his demands that Herod had no right to remain married to Herodias (Mark 6:14-18)?

Don't forget the polygamist (with his six wives and many children). Does emotion, fairness, and justice demand that he stay with his wives and children?

6. "1 Corinthians 7:20 says, 'Let every man abide in the same calling wherein he was called'; thus one can continue in the marriage he is in when he obeys the gospel."

The context (vv. 12-24) is not talking about adulterous marriages, but being married to unbelievers. The question being dealt with is whether the believer (new convert) should leave his/her unbelieving mate. Paul's answer is no. Continue in that marriage. If 1 Corinthians 7:20 is talking about adulterous marriages, it also includes polygamy and homosexuality. In fact, it would include every type of sin (e.g. idolatry).

7. "Adultery is not the sexual act, but the divorce and remarriage for Matthew 19:9 says that he who puts away and remarries commits adultery."

That is not the meaning of the word nor how it is used in this or any other passage. He commits adultery when he remarries for marriage suggests that there will be sexual activity. If we were to use that same kind of reasoning on Matthew 5:32, we would have to conclude that one who is put away (innocently) is guilty of adultery. Thus, adultery would mean to be put away without a cause. No, in reality the text assumes much more (that she remarries and cohabits).

8. "The second marriage is not adultery if the first marriage is ended, for adultery involves those who are married."

Matthew 19:9 says otherwise. Notice that the man puts away his wife (thus, the first marriage is ended) and marries another (the second marriage is contracted) and he still commits adultery. The same is true of Matthew 5:32, Mark 10:9-10, and Luke 16:18.

9. "All (including the adulterer) have a right to be married (1 Cor. 7:9)."

No, not all have a right to be married. The man who puts away his wife (for a cause other than fornication) doesn't have that right (Matt. 19:9). The one who is put away doesn't have that right (Matt. 5:32; 19:9). What about those six women married to one man: do they all have a right to be married to him?

10. "If separation is required, then salvation is dependent on works of merit and not grace."

Separation is no more a work of merit than baptism or any other act of obedience. Must the idolater quit his idolatry? Is that a work of merit? Or, does grace mean he can keep his idol? Must the murderer, drunkard, and gambler quit their sins? Don't forget to apply the same to the homosexual and polygamist.

11. "A point often overlooked in Romans 7:1-4 is that verse 4 says that remarriage is allowed."

Yes, remarriage is allowed, but it is when death had severed the first marriage. If it is allowed before then, why is she called an adulteress (v. 3)?

12. "'Committeth adultery' is aorist present (indicating point or completed action rather than progressive action) rather than the present indicative."

The scholars say that the aorist present is a rare use of the present tense. "This use is a distinct departure from the prevailing use of the present tense to denote action in progress" (Dana and Mantey, *A Manual Grammar of the Greek New Testament,* 184). Robertson says the same thing (*A Grammar of the Greek New Testament in Light of Historical Research,* 864). This argument is an assumption with no proof. If we were to grant the point that it is aorist present, it would not limit the adultery to the first unlawful sexual act. "The aorist present sets forth an event as now occurring" (Dana and Mantey, 184). The event occurs as the speaker is speaking. Jesus referred to the future when a man would put away his wife and marry another. If aorist present is used, the future putting away and remarriage would result in an act of adultery even as Jesus spoke. Absurd!

13. "1 Corinthians 7:10-11 says that the married couple should not depart."

That passage also forbids remarriage! If that passage forbids adulterers separating it would also forbid the homosexual and polygamist separating.

14. "David committed adultery with Bathsheba and continued to live with her."

Uriah, her first husband (as far as we know), was killed. His death severed the bond (Rom. 7:2-3), thus allowing her the right to remarry. However, David had more than one wife. If this argument proves it is right for those today living in adultery to continue to live together, it proves the right of multiple wives.

15. "We can continue relationships that began in sin. For example: a child conceived out of wedlock. The parent-child relationship can continue."

The parent-child relationship is not parallel to the husband-wife (in adultery). The parent-child relationship does not involve sin; the husband-wife relationship (in the case of adultery) is sin.

In the former, fornication was the sin and it must cease. In the latter, adultery is the sin and it must cease.

16. "In John 4 Jesus did not require the Samaritan woman to separate."

Jesus said that the man she had at the time was not her husband (v. 18). If this text proves anything about not separating, it would prove the legitimacy of living together without marriage. Who can accept it?

17. "In Matthew 18:23-25 the man was forgiven of his debt and not required to pay any back."

Again, it is not a question of *restitution, paying back* or *undoing the past.* It is a question of *ceasing the sin.* If Matthew 18 proves that adulterers do not have to separate, it would also prove that polygamists do not have to separate.

Consequences

To contend that adulterers do not have to separate in order to have fellowship with God and faithful brethren, one must be willing to face the obvious and serious consequences.

1. The polygamist can continue with his wives and still be saved.

2. The homosexual can continue in his marriage and still be saved.

3. Either the Christian is released from the law of Christ or God allows him to sin without any consequences.

Questions

Verses to remember: "For Herod himself had sent forth and laid hold upon John, and bound him in prison for Herodias' sake, his brother Philip's wife: for he had married her. For John had said unto Herod, It is not lawful for thee to have thy brother's wife" (Mark 6:17-18).

Discussion

1. Discuss the emotional plea that this issue has. _____

2. Discuss the consequences that the position under review has. _____

3. Discuss the meaning of repentance. _____

4. Discuss how that a greater emotional plea could be made for the first marriage that was destroyed than for the second or third marriage. _____

5. Discuss whether or not it is fair for a person to be required to live a celibate life. _____

True or False

_____ 1. Adultery refers to the first unlawful sexual act only.

_____ 2. Baptism washes away all sin.

_____ 3. There is no command, example, or necessary inference that demands adulterers to separate.

_____ 4. Repentance involves ceasing the sin.

_____ 5. "Committeth adultery" (Matt. 19:9) is present tense which denotes continual action.

Find the Passage

1. "Bring forth therefore fruits meet for repentance." _____

2. "Mortify therefore your members which are upon the earth; fornication, ... in the which ye also walked some time, when ye lived in them." _____

3. "And the times of this ignorance God winked at; but now commandeth all men everywhere to repent." _____

4. "And lest, when I come again, my God will humble me among you, and that I shall bewail many which have sinned already, and have not repented of the uncleanness and fornication...." _____

5. "He answered and said, I will not: but afterward he repented and went." _____

Answer in a Few Words

1. Can the second marriage be adultery if the first marriage has ended? _____

2. Give a command, example, and necessary inference that tells the adulterers to separate. _____

3. How would you answer the argument that "committeth adultery" does not mean continual action? _____

4. What are the two basic views that say that no separation is required? _____

5. What is the real issue in this lesson? _____

Multiple Choice

_____ 1. The question at hand is (a) restitution, (b) cessation of sin, (c) undoing the past.

_____ 2. (a) All, (b) some, (c) none have/has a right to remarry.

_____ 3. Adultery means (a) the first unlawful sexual act, (b) to break wedlock or the covenant, (c) to have unlawful intercourse with another's wife.

_____ 4. An unscriptural marriage before baptism (a) is sanctified, (b) is still unscriptural after baptism.

_____ 5. The context of 1 Corinthians 7:20 discusses (a) adulterous marriages, (b) a believer being married to an unbeliever, (c) any and all relationships.

Fill in the Blank

1. If the position under review is true, either the Christian is _____ from the _____ of Christ or God _____ him to sin _____ _____.

2. The question about repentance is not _____ or _____ the past, but _____ the sin.

3. Most of the arguments and quibbles can be answered easily when we remember that what will work for the adulterer will also work for the _____ and the _____.

4. Every passage that commands _____ is a passage that commands _____.

5. The present tense which is used in Matthew 19:9 indicates _____ action.

Lesson 13

A Review, a Look at a Few Basic Points to Remember and Conclusion

A verse to remember: *"And I say unto you, Whosoever shall put away his wife, except it be for fornication, and shall marry another, committeth adultery: and whoso marrieth her which is put away doth commit adultery" (Matt. 19:9).*

This chapter does not address any new material but is designed to review and summarize all of the previous chapters. The reader is encouraged to reread (or at least scan) chapters 1-12 before finishing this review.

Let us not forget that the standard we must use in determining what is right or wrong on the issue of divorce and remarriage is not the family situation, human emotions or what some well known brother may think. Rather, it is what the text (the word of God) says.

What Matthew 19:9 Teaches

Look back to Lesson 4 for a discussion of Matthew 19:9 and the parallel texts: Matthew 5:32, Mark 10:11-12, and Luke 16:18.

1. Divorce. Jesus does not command or require divorce, but it is permitted under certain conditions. There are many reasons why one might obtain a divorce (incompatibility, personal dislike, burning the bread, irreconcilable differences and even fornication). However, Jesus allowed only one cause — fornication, whether or not there will be any remarriage.

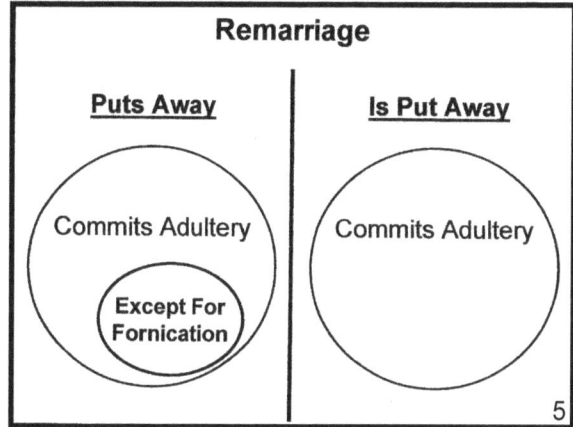

2. Remarriage. In the case of remarriage after divorce, the blanket rule is that it is adultery. The one exception is when one puts away his or her mate for fornication. Carefully consider chart 5.

If the one who puts away remarries, it is adultery if the divorce was for some cause other than fornication. It is not adultery if the divorce was for fornication. If the put away one remarries, it is adultery whether the cause be fornication or not.

Matthew 19:9 contains two complete clauses joined by "and." The one who puts away (exception: fornication) and remarries commits adultery *and* when the one who is put away remarries, he commits adultery.

Obviously, when the put away one (whether for fornication or another reason) remarries, it is adultery. When no fornication is involved, remarriage for both partners is adultery. It does not matter which person remarries first, both remarriages are adultery.

Who Can Marry?

This point was discussed in detail in Lesson 5. The question concerns who has a scriptural right to marry.

1. One who has never been married (Matt. 19:4-5; Heb. 13:4; 1 Cor. 7:2, 28).
2. One whose mate is dead (Rom. 7:3).
3. One who puts away his/her mate for fornication (Matt. 19:9).
4. Those reconciling (1 Cor. 7:11).

If any more are to be added to this list, there must also be a passage that justifies that remarriage.

The Difference in the *Marriage* and the *Bond*

This point was discussed in detail in Lesson 5.

1. The confusion. When we fail to make a distinction in the *marriage* and the *bond*, our terminology becomes quite confusing. The concept of many is that if one is no longer married, he is no longer bound. A lot is said about being married "in the eyes of men" and married "in the eyes of God." Thus, a distinction is made between marriage (and divorce) that is "real" and "legal." We are told if God approves, it is "real," but if he disapproves it is not "real" but only a "legal" divorce or remarriage. All of this merely confuses the marriage and the bond.

2. There is a difference. This is obvious from the fact that in Romans 7:2, 3 the woman is *bound* to her first husband even though she is *married* to her second husband. Marriage is a relationship entered into by agreement and compliance with civil law. The bond is a covenant with God that joins us to our mate. Thus, a divorce (scriptural or not) is really a divorce. Likewise, a marriage (scriptural or not) is really a marriage. The thing that keeps one from remarrying is that he/she is still bound (Rom. 7:2-3).

All Men (Aliens and Christians) Are Amenable to the Law of Christ

This was discussed in Lesson 11. While there are those who believe that the alien sinner is not subject to the law of Christ, the Bible plainly shows that the alien is amenable to the law of Christ.

1. Christ has universal authority (Matt. 28:18; Acts 17:30-31; Rev. 1:5).

2. The gospel is addressed to all men (Matt. 28:19; Mark 16:15).

3. The alien is guilty of sin — which shows that he has violated the law of Christ (1 John 3:4; Rom. 4:15).

4. In Matthew 19:9 Jesus applied his law to "whosoever."

Conclusion

This writer sincerely hopes that when the reader lays this book aside to pursue other studies, that he will do so with a better and clearer understanding of what the text says about divorce and remarriage. Continue to study the subject. Never let this book or any other written by man become the final authority. Pursue questions and arguments that are not dealt with in this book. Continue to discuss the issues of divorce and remarriage with others (even with those with whom you may disagree). And, as discussions continue on for years to come, keep an open mind. Joseph Joubert once said, "It is better to debate a question without settling it than to settle a question without debating it."

This book has tried to set forth the simple teaching of the New Testament on divorce and remarriage and answer the objections and show the consequences of various positions brethren take. When those "alternative" positions are shown to be false, the truth shines forth even dearer. Henry Kissinger once said, "The absence of alternatives clears the mind marvelously."

NOTES

Questions

A verse to remember: "And I say unto you, Whosoever shall put away his wife, except it be for fornication, and shall marry another, committeth adultery: and whoso marrieth her which is put away doth commit adultery" (Matt. 19:9).

Discussion

1. Why do the people of God need to discuss the issues pertaining to divorce and remarriage? _____

2. Why is this subject so controversial? _____

3. Discuss how some people use family situations, emotions, or some well known brother as standards in determining what is right on this subject. _____

4. Who has the right to marry? _____

5. What stood out most in your mind about this study of divorce and remarriage? _____

True or False

_____ 1. Some put away ones can remarry.

_____ 2. It is possible to be bound to one and married to another.

_____ 3. Matthew 19:9 was addressed to "whosoever."

_____ 4. There is a difference in a marriage (and divorce) that is "real" and one that is "legal."

_____ 5. Jesus gave only one cause for divorce: fornication.

Find the Passage

1. "But I say unto you, That whosoever shall put away his wife, saving for the cause of fornication, causeth her to commit adultery: and whosoever shall marry her that is divorced committeth adultery." _____

2. "For the woman which hath an husband is bound by the law to her husband so long as he liveth.... So then if, while her husband liveth, she be married to another man, she shall be called an adulteress...." _____

3. "Go ye into all the world, and preach the gospel to every creature." _____

4. "All power is given unto me in heaven and in earth." _____

5. "Because the law worketh wrath: for where no law is, there is no transgression." _____

Answer in a Few Words

1. Does God allow divorce for any cause when there is no intention of remarrying? _____
   _____

2. If Jack puts away Jill for burning the bread and he remarries, does Jill commit adultery if she remarries?_____

3. What does "amenable" mean? _____

4. List those who are authorized to marry. _____
   _____

5. List some who are not authorized to marry. _____
   _____

Multiple Choice

_____ 1. The gospel is addressed (a) only to the alien, (b) only to the Christian, (c) to both the alien and the Christian.

_____ 2. If God does not approve of a marriage (a) it is not real, (b) it is marriage only in the "eyes of men," (c) it is still a marriage.

_____ 3. (a) Only the one who puts away his mate for fornication, (b) Only the one who is put away, (c) Both the one who puts away and the one who is put away has/have the right to remarry.

_____ 4. Our standard must be (a) whatever the family situation is, (b) our emotions, (c) some well known brother, (d) this book, (e) the word of God.

_____ 5. Divorce is allowed (a) for any cause, (b) if there is no intention to remarry, (c) only for the cause of fornication.

Fill in the Blank

1. If the alien is not under the _____ of Christ, he could not be guilty of _____, for sin is the transgression of the _____.

2. The thing that keeps one from remarrying is that he is still _____.

3. We must not allow any book written by _____ to become the final _____.

4. Jesus has _____ authority.

5. Romans 7:2-3 shows a woman can be _____ to her first husband while she is _____ to the second husband.

Appendix

What Does Marry "Only in the Lord" Mean (1 Cor. 7:39)?

There are three basic positions taken on this. (1) Some think that it means that widows, if they remarry, must marry Christians. (2) Others think that it merely means that she must remarry "according to the will of God." (3) Still, others think that it means that she is to remarry a Christian, but it is limited to the "present distress."

This writer believes that this last position is correct. The "present distress" (v. 26) seems to have been some type of short, severe persecution (v. 29). It was a difficult period for any Christian, but especially difficult for those who were married. Their families would suffer too as they were persecuted. That is why Paul said "It is good for a man not to touch a woman" (v. 2) and "I would that all men were even as I myself" (v. 7). Likewise, during this period, it would be a great difficulty upon the widow if she remarried an unbeliever. Thus, during this time, she must marry "only in the Lord" (a Christian).

Can One Be Reconciled to His/Her "Put Away" Mate?

Again, we must keep in mind the distinction of the *marriage* and the *bond* (Rom. 7:3-4). While this couple are no longer married, the "put away" one is still bound to his/her first mate. The "put away" one has no right to any other but the one who put him/her away. Thus, the answer is yes. They can be reconciled.

1 Corinthians 7:10-11 plainly shows that when there has been a divorce that the couple can be reconciled. According to this text when one does not have a right to remarry another, he must either (1) be reconciled or (2) remain unmarried. If the reconciliation does not apply to the put away fornicator (as some have contended) then the requirement for him to remain unmarried would not apply.

It is argued that Matthew 19:9b says that whoever marries the put away one commits adultery. If there was reconciliation, the first husband would be marrying a "put away" one and thus sinning we are told. Look carefully at Matthew 19:9b. It is implied that the "whosoever" that marries the "put away" one is someone other than her first husband. He is not even under consideration! When she is reconciled to him, she is not marrying another, but him (her first husband).

Some have argued that reconciliation is not permitted because the "put away" fornicator is an adulteress. Suppose that the divorce was for some cause other than fornication and neither one was an adulterer or adulteress. Could they be reconciled? If yes, the contender must think that Matthew 19:9b only applies to "put away" fornicators, meaning that any other "put away" ones could remarry. If no, being an adulteress has nothing to do with reconciliation being permitted.

Does 2 Corinthians 6:14 Refer to Marriage?

"Unequally yoked" means to pull together with an unbeliever in serving sin. The context will bear that out. In verse 14 Paul raises the question about the fellowship with unrighteousness and darkness and in verse 16 idols. The next chapter instructs us to cleanse ourselves from all filthiness of flesh and spirit (v. 1).

This "yoke" does not refer to the marriage for in 1 Corinthians 7:12-13 Paul said that the marriage of a Christian to a non-Christian was not to be ended, but to continue. In our context, this yoke is to be broken (v. 17). Thus, they are not the same.

Are There Other Consequences to the Argument That Says That Matthew 19:9 Condemns "Divorce AND Remarriage" and Not Mere Divorce?

If this passage only condemns divorce *and* remarriage and not mere divorce, then only divorce *and* remarriage (for fornication) is allowed. Mere divorce (for fornication) would not be allowed. One couldn't divorce for fornication

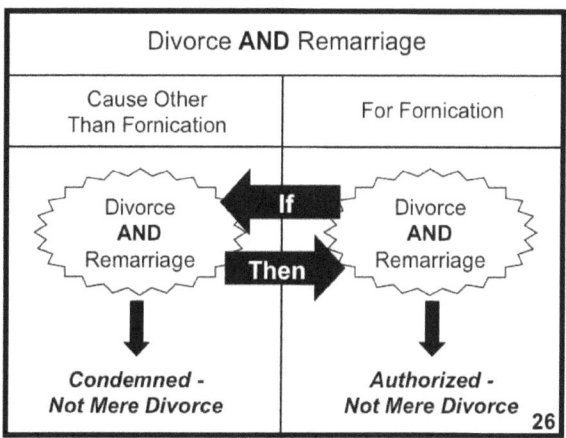

unless there were plans to remarry. Consider chart 26 (page 113).

What About a "Put Away" One Whose Mate Dies, Can He Remarry?

Yes, for death severed the bond (Rom. 7:2-3). The woman of Romans 7 was bound to her husband only as long as he lived.

Is 1 Corinthians 7:11 "If She Depart" — Active or Passive, Past or Future?

There are various interpretations. Some think it is active future. The meaning would be "if she separates contrary to Christ's command." Others think it is active past, "If she has already separated." Still others think it may be passive future, "if she is left." The word translated "depart" (*chōristhē*) is first aorist, passive, subjunctive. "Whether we take the meaning of this subjunctive as passive or active really does not make much difference" (Spiros Zodhiates, *May I Divorce And Remarry? — An Exegetical Commentary on 1 Cor. 7*, 117). "The verb in Greek is chooristhee, the third person singular first aorist subjunctive passive with middle meaning of choorizoo" (she separates herself — DVR) (*Ibid.*, 123). H.A.W. Meyer agrees with Zodhiates saying, "*But in case she should perhaps even be separated* (have separated herself); in this Paul is not granting something in the way of exception, as though the preceding injunction were not to be taken too strictly ... but he supposes a future case, which will probably arise notwithstanding the commandment of the Lord just adduced" (*Meyer's Commentary on the New Testament,* VI: 157).

I think Zodhiates and Meyer are probably correct. Though passive in form, it is probably active or middle in meaning. That seems to fit the context. Verse 10 forbids her departing (a thing that she does or does not do). Verse 11 says if she does that, here is what she must do. The matter of remaining "unmarried" or being "reconciled" is the only thing that can be done for any divorcee who can't remarry (whether one puts away or is put away).

Divorce and Remarriage and Fellowship

The attitude of many is that issues that surround divorce and remarriage are so difficult and since we all disagree we should let the matter alone and let each individual settle it for himself. If so, shall we ignore those who live contrary to the teaching of Matthew 19:9? Shall we allow people to divorce and remarry and live in adultery and never say a word? Shall we let the preachers and teachers who encourage such relationships pass without notice?

When there are opposing views on divorce and remarriage, somebody is wrong! The question is: Are the issues of divorce and remarriage of such significance to break fellowship? Let's consider a few simple points.

1. We are not to fellowship sin or those in sin (Eph. 5:11; 1 Cor. 5; 2 Cor. 6:14).

2. Fellowship must be with those who "walk in the light" or abide in the "doctrine of Christ" (1 John 1:7, 2 John 9).

Thus, we can't fellowship (1) the adulterer (1 Cor. 5). Those who divorce and remarry contrary to the teaching of Christ cannot enter into or continue in the fellowship with God's people. Neither can we fellowship (2) one who teaches error. The church at Thyatira was rebuked for continuing to tolerate those whose teachings lead to fornication (Rev. 2:18-21). Those who disturb congregational peace by their teaching must be marked (Rom. 16:17; Tit. 3:10). Those whose teaching causes others to become adulterers and adulteresses cannot be fellowshipped anymore than the adulterer or adulteress themselves (cf. 2 Tim. 2:17-18). There are brethren who have publicly taught an erroneous position on divorce and remarriage that caused others to either enter into or continue in an adulterous marriage. They are not guiltless when this happens. There is just as much harm done by those who teach privately and again disturb congregational peace or cause others to enter into or continue in adultery. This often happens when a man goes to a place to hold a meeting. He may not say anything about his position in the pulpit, but as he goes from house to house eating and visiting with the brethren, they may ask him what he thinks about divorce and remarriage. He then has an opportunity to teach his erroneous views. Another factor to consider is that the doctrine may have very serious consequences (e.g. that the alien is not subject to the law of Christ).

We must point out that there is a difference between one who merely holds a different view and one who is teaching and advocating that view (publicly or privately). I am not ready to mark every brother off the first time I detect that we are not in agreement on divorce and remarriage. There must be time to study the issue. Let us exhaust all efforts to study the issue before we draw lines of fellowship. However, it is a different story when he begins to teach his position.

Some have tried to parallel the divorce and remarriage issues to the covering issue, the war question and differences over the qualifications of elders. Even those who try to make these parallel don't really believe they are. If one had a daughter to change her mind and practice on the covering, it would not be near as disturbing as if she had entered into an unscriptural marriage.

More Arguments on the Mental Divorce Position

In Lesson 8 we dealt with a number of arguments that are made to justify the mental divorce position. Here we answer several more.

1. "The word 'and' (Greek: *kai*) in Matthew 19:9 can be translated 'or' as it is in Matthew 7:10 and 2 Corinthians 13:1."

Earlier in chapter 8 we showed that "and" does not mean "or" in Matthew 19:9. In Matthew 7:10 it is a combination of *ē* and *kai* and not merely *kai*. It is the Greek word *ē* that is translated "*or*." Nestles interlinear translates *ē* as "or" and *kai* as "also." In 2 Corinthians 13:1 it is used to connect numerals which is not to be equated with its use of connecting words and phrases as it is used in Matthew 19:9. Again, Nestles text translates *kai* as "and': There is no translation, to my knowledge, that translates *kai* as "or" in Matthew 19:9.

2. "'Divorce' means to repudiate or send away, thus it is a mental thing and not just a legal process."

While "repudiate" and "sending away" may be a part of divorce, that is not all that it means. 1 Corinthians 7:10-11 (which we have already shown to be discussing divorce, chapter 7) shows that divorce ends the marriage. The marriage that *begins* legally, must also *end* legally. Even the concept of "sending away" involves more than something "mental." Divorce, like marriage, is something observable.

3. "The 'whosoever' (that has a right to remarry) of Matthew 19:9 is all inclusive with these exceptions: (1) The put away fornicator, (2) One who puts away for a cause other than fornication, (3) Those who play the waiting game. Thus, the woman who is put away unjustly by her husband who then remarries another is included."

The "whosoever" refers to the one who puts away and not the put away one. If we use the above reasoning, why not include the woman who is put away when her husband doesn't remarry? The argument assumes that which must be proven.

4. "In Matthew 1:19 Joseph was going to put away Mary 'privily.' Thus, the putting away would have to be mental."

"Privily" does not suggest that it was without legal requirements. Under the regulations of Deuteronomy 24 it was customary to specify a cause. In this case it seems that Joseph was planning to put her away without specifying a cause, for he didn't want to make her a public spectacle. This is the meaning of "privily." Notice that he was "minded" already, though he had not yet put her away "privily." Thus, "privily" involves more than a mental act.

5. "In Matthew 19:6, 'let not man put asunder' means man cannot (it is impossible) sever (really) a marriage unless fornication is involved. Thus, when a man puts away his wife for a cause other than fornication, the marriage has not really been severed until he remarries another. When he does that, the divorce is real and the put away wife can remarry."

"Let not" does not mean "cannot." Why would Jesus say 'let not man put asunder" if it is impossible to do that? Verses 7-8 show that the issue was what was "lawful," not what was possible.

6. "If a put away one cannot later mentally put away an adulterous mate, then God requires that one to be bound to an adulterous mate."

Remember that the "bond" is not only to your mate, but is also with God (Prov. 2:17; Mal. 2:14-ff; Rom. 7:2-3). The adulterous one (that has been put away) is no longer your mate, even though you are bound by God's law (cf. chapter 5). The text says that "whoso marrieth her which is put away doth commit adultery" (Matt. 19:9). There is no Bible authority for the put away one to mentally put his/her mate away and marry another.

7. "The Bible says that there is one baptism, yet when one is baptized into the Baptist Church (out of harmony with God's law) that does not mean he can't turn and be baptized in harmony with God's law. Likewise, there is one divorce (scripturally). Yet, if one is divorced (unscripturally) that doesn't mean he can't turn around and divorce scripturally."

The contention is comparing apples and oranges. If this argument proves anything it would prove that the one who puts away his wife (unscripturally) would have a right to remarry if his put away wife remarried before he did. While many will accept that consequence, not all of the mental divorce advocates are ready to accept that. Baptism and divorce are not parallel in all respects. If they were, we could argue that a scriptural divorce is allowed, but not commanded. Thus, a scriptural baptism is allowed, but not commanded. Oops, that won't work.

8. "Forbidding to marry is a doctrine of the devil (1 Tim. 4:1ff)."

That contention could be used to prove that all have a right to remarry. That would allow the guilty party and the one put away where no fornication is involved and the one who puts away for a cause other than fornication to remarry. The fact is that there is not one of the advocates of this argument that doesn't teach that there is someone who can't remarry.

9. "We all agree that some 'put away' ones can remarry: (1) One whose mate dies (even though he is put away) is free to remarry. (2) One who is being reconciled. Now, Matthew 19:9 allows for these though it says nothing about them. Likewise, it says nothing about mental divorce by one who has been put away by an adulterous mate, but it is allowed."

This argument is based upon silence. It is assumed that something is allowed since nothing is said about it. Matthew 19:9 nor any other passage allows for things about which it says nothing. Other passages (not Matt. 19:9) speak of death and reconciliation (Rom. 7:2-3; 1 Cor. 7:10-11).

10. "Every man should have his own wife (1 Cor. 7:2). That includes the one who has been put away."

Should the guilty party have a right to remarry? Should the one put away, where no fornication or remarriage has taken place, have a right to remarry? This reasoning would prove that no one is forbidden to remarry. There would be no such thing as an adulterous marriage. Also, to have a right to one's "own wife" does not suggest a right to remarry another. This passage would prove that he only as a right to the first mate.

11. "If it is a 'real' divorce, it means the party has a right to remarry."

A "real" divorce (as the mental divorce advocates would call it) does not grant a right for remarriage. The guilty party has been put away by a "real" divorce. Can he remarry? A "real" divorce did not grant such a right in 1 Corinthians 7:10-11 or Matthew 19:9.

12. "It is the adultery that gives the right to remarry and not who does the putting away or who is put away."

It is true that divorce does not grant the right to remarry. Fornication must be the cause. However, Matthew 19:9 does make a distinction in one who *puts away* and one who *is put away*.

13. "If a put away one cannot remarry, then a man could take off to Reno and get a quickie divorce and remarry before his first wife even knows he is gone. That would leave her in a position where she can't remarry."

This is a play on emotions, which proves nothing about what the Bible says. This could be turned around. Suppose the man takes off to Reno, gets the quickie divorce, but never remarries. Is his poor first wife to live celibate the rest of her life?

14. "Concerning the 'put away' one having a right to mentally put away his first mate and remarry: The civil 'divorce' is not the real one. Divine law supercedes human law. Civil authority and law has not always been necessary for divorce or marriage. Thus, a lack of civil authority (for a put away one to divorce his mate) does not mean it cannot be done."

This assumes that there is a difference in divorce that is "real" (approved by God) and that which is "not real" (not approved by God). See chapter 5. The real question is not one of civil authority for the put away one to turn and put away his mate, but one of Biblical authority.

www.ingramcontent.com/pod-product-compliance
Lightning Source LLC
Chambersburg PA
CBHW080940040426
42444CB00015B/3383